Ladies Who Lunch

A play

Tudor Gates

Samuel French — London
New York - Toronto - Hollywood

© 1999 BY DRUMBEAT LTD

Rights of Performance by Amateurs are controlled by Samuel French Ltd, 52 Fitzroy Street, London W1P 6JR, and they, or their authorized agents, issue licences to amateurs on payment of a fee. **It is an infringement of the Copyright to give any performance or public reading of the play before the fee has been paid and the licence issued.**

The Royalty Fee indicated below is subject to contract and subject to variation at the sole discretion of Samuel French Ltd.

> Basic fee for each and every
> performance by amateurs   Code M
> in the British Isles

The Professional Rights in this play are controlled by Eric Glass Ltd, 28 Berkeley Square, London, W1X 6HD

The publication of this play does not imply that it is necessarily available for performance by amateurs or professionals, either in the British Isles or Overseas. Amateurs and professionals considering a production are strongly advised in their own interests to apply to the appropriate agents for written consent before starting rehearsals or booking a theatre or hall.

ISBN 0 573 01853 7

Please see page iv for further copyright information

SYNOPSIS OF SCENES

It is late Autumn in England and New York, although already cold there. It is early Summer in Sydney.

ACT I

SCENE 1	London, morning
SCENE 2	London, later that morning
SCENE 3	Sydney, evening some days later
SCENE 4	New York, evening about a month later
SCENE 5	London, morning some weeks later

ACT II

SCENE 1	London, continues from Act I, Scene 5
SCENE 2	New York, morning two days later
SCENE 3	New York, midday the next day
SCENE 4	Sydney, morning two days later
SCENE 5	New York, afternoon the same day
SCENE 6	Sydney, morning the next day
SCENE 7	New York, afternoon the same day
SCENE 8	London, evening the same day

AUTHOR'S NOTE

This play was written for the British Telecom Biennial and played simultaneously at thirty-nine different amateur theatres in Great Britain—and one in Fort Worth, Florida—during the latter part of October 1998.

I was fortunate enough to have the opportunity of conducting a number of workshops in the preceding months and then to see six performances of the participants; in Formby, Wells, the Isles of Sheppey and Wight, Sheerness and London—the latter of which I directed myself with a company drawn from British Telecom staff.

It was not an easy play to put on, with three different sets, some demanding roles, and a host of lightning costume changes, but the companies responded to the challenges brilliantly.

Thus I have seen decor varying from one set with changing backgrounds, to three adjacent settings; from a multi-level complex to a revolving stage: I found each production offered its own original contributions. The prologue was also a test of ingenuity. One company produced a professional-looking video; another showed slides. One company thought laterally and opted for a radio version, while others played it live, but in quite different ways.

The same went for the actors; no two performances were identical. The role of Joane was not always the show-stopper; I saw some excellent Rachels—one marvellous, quirky performance—and of course Lady Amelia holds the whole piece together. There were some brilliant Amelias.

Similarly, I saw a bewildering display of Gerrys, some amazingly different interpretations of Wallis, and a (not literally) stout succession of maids.

The men were uniformly excellent even though, rather unusually, they were supporting the distaff side. The relationships of the three couples, each quite unlike the others, were often beautifully drawn—vital to the play's success. Every Sir John had something the others did not, and the same went for Ken and Harry. They are meaty, if not wordy, roles.

So I found the whole experience a tremendously satisfying one. There is a serious theme to the play, although it is a comedy, and many of the companies donated their profits to appropriate charities. Above all, for me, audiences laughed and enjoyed the piece. No author can ask for more.

If you are planning a production, do please invite me to see it. If I can come, I will, and if I can't, then please accept my apologies now and my very best wishes for a great success.

TG

A NOTE ON THE AUSTRALIAN IDIOM

They sometimes make up names in Australia by contracting others—"Noelene" for example, or as here, "Joane". It is not Joanne. "Joane" allows for two strangulated vowel sounds.

The following is a glossary of terms which may be unfamiliar to the reader:

Banana bender	Someone from Queensland
Barrack	To be in support of
Bludger	A heavy
Bondi tram	One that doesn't stop
Boomer	Big
Bull dust	Dried excreta
Bush pig	An ugly woman of doubtful morals
Bushranger	A crook
Cark it	To die
Comfort station	Toilet
Crook	Sick or damaged
Dill	An idiot
Dingbat	Someone who can't understand
Dingo	A wild dog that has been known to eat babies
Drongo	A witless individual
Eat the bum off a low flying duck	Be hungry
Galah	A fool
Good oil	Information
Hook	A confidence trick
Home and hosed	Arrived safely
Larrikin	Someone who throws his weight about
Living on the boat	Free and unencumbered
Lurk	A scheme

Mallee bull	A creature that crashes wildly around
Nong	A stupid person
Rafferty's rules	Anything goes
Root	A stud
Roustabout	Philanderer
Salvo	Member of the Salvation Army
Sheila	A female
Spit the dummy	End something
Stubbie	A squat bottle of beer

"Greenmail" is not a specifically Australian term but it seems not to be generally understood. When someone seeks to take over a company, they buy the shares, which then rise in value. If they fail to win total control, they still have a major influence. The only way to get rid of them is to buy them out. So the raiders make a huge profit. It is a form of blackmail—"greenmail" because of the colour of dollars.

PRODUCTION NOTE

The set is both simple and complex—as simple or as complex as you want it to be. Initially it is a grand drawing room in Belgravia but will later represent the living-room of an apartment in Sydney and a penthouse in New York.

The possibilities are obviously endless. Since the action of the play will always make it clear where we are, the piece could almost be played on a bare stage. If you have funds and a brilliant lighting designer, you can draw gasps from your audiences with, say, the magnificent view of Sydney Bridge and the Opera House from Darling Point, and a breathtaking panorama of sparkling Manhattan. In London, it doesn't even have to be Belgravia, if you would rather look along the Thames towards Charing Cross and Big Ben. Each of these views could be from picture windows, placed L, R and C across the back wall—or from a single window—or the window could be the audience.

There are no doors. Everyone exits and enters through the wings R and L.

The furniture should be as simple as possible so that it fits into all three sets, with any adjustments required. The two sets not in present view, if you are splitting the stage, will of course darken into obscurity. It might be easier just to move the furniture, giving it three distinct settings for the different locations. A revolve obviously makes life more simple. Appropriate music will also help set the scenes (e.g. "didgeridoo" theme for Australia). Please note also that telephone rings differ in different countries.

ACKNOWLEDGEMENTS

I would like to thank my stockbroker friend, Edgar, for guiding me through the intricacies of international high finance, and my niece, Debra, for her advice on the colourful Australian vernacular. I am also indebted to John Hague, the Project Manager, and all my erstwhile colleagues at British Telecom for their valiant efforts—both on and off the stage.

TG

ACT I

Prologue

The purpose of the prologue is to set the theme of the play. It can be performed in a number of ways. The excerpt that follows can be filmed and shown on a screen, or recorded on video and played on a monitor. This can be removed, or left on stage as a TV set. If none of these is feasible, it can be slightly adapted to play on radio, on set, as a brief curtain-raiser. The scene can also be played live, with the actors crossing the stage or entering from the stalls, in which case two actors need to be added, or the roles of the commentators doubled

If using a film clip, we show a few seconds of African children, looking helplessly at the camera, before going to a close-up of a safari-suited female reporter, Kate Glass

Kate And in the meantime, civil war continues to rage out here, and the population starves. Children die, while mothers look on helplessly. And all we who have to endure watching this can ask is: what is the West going to do about it? Kate Glass, News at One, in West Africa.

The scene on film that follows is a posh hotel, with the members of a charitable organisation, dressed to the nines, arriving for lunch. Peter Rain, microphone in hand, is the commentator

Peter Well, Kate, here in London, at the Grand Carlton Hotel of all places, someone is trying to do something about it. The Women's International Committee for the Save Our Starving Campaign, will at a luncheon here today promise to try and raise a million dollars for the fund—a tall order, you might think, but not perhaps when you consider the social fire-power of some of the ladies of the Committee.

A stout lady in furs preens for the cameras

That's the Dowager Duchess of Heckmondshire, just arriving, whose family owns many hundreds of thousands of acres in Scotland, and that's Mrs Joane Stocks, wife of the so-called Wizard of Oz, Kenneth Stocks, reputedly the second richest man in the Antipodes.

We see Joane, one of our leading characters, wave a hand towards the cameras. She is around forty, a bit blowsy perhaps, but exceptionally well-dressed. She is extrovert in personality, and has a cheerful smile. She is followed by two other leading members of the cast, Rachel Milchan and Lady Amelia Sasson. Rachel is in her mid-thirties, attractive but a bit mousy, an American Jewish princess. Amelia is forty, elegant in speech, dress and manner. Her gentleness belies a core of hard steel

And here's another visitor from abroad, Rachel Milchan. Her husband is the famous, some say infamous, bond-broker in New York, who must be worth billions! And there's still some money left in the UK, witness the arrival of Lady Amelia, second wife of the fabulously rich Sir John Sasson, a power on the London Stock Exchange. Lady Amelia chairs the Committee and is well known in charitable circles for getting things done—they say she's a real dynamo! Believe me, if she says today they're going to raise a million dollars for those unfortunate children, then somehow or the other, and no matter what it takes, they will! (*He signs off*) Peter Rain, outside the Grand Carlton Hotel in London, for News at One.

Black-out

Scene 1

The Sassons' drawing-room in Belgravia, London. Morning

As the Curtain *rises, Lady Amelia and Sir John are having a row. John is in his fifties, probably balding, a man of considerable charisma. He is in a state of angry irritation. Amelia is calm and in control—always!*

John Let them starve!
Amelia Don't be so theatrical.
John I mean it.
Amelia Nonsense. She's your daughter.
John Not any more, she's not. Not unless she does what I say.
Amelia Isn't that just a trifle Victorian, darling? Gerry is twenty-one.
John Geraldine. Her name's Geraldine. And she's become a blasted hippy!
Amelia John, hippies went out when you were young. She has—punk tendencies—that's all.
John All? A blasted diamond stud in her nose and a ring in her lip? What next?
Amelia I believe a pierced navel is the in-thing.
John (*snorting*) Some of us still have standards.

Amelia (*soothing*) Of course we do.
John And I have a position in the City.
Amelia I know. And that's what all this is really about, isn't it?
John That girl was brilliant at University—brilliant!
Amelia She just wants to do her own thing. Not everyone wants to carry on the family business.
John (*stubbornly*) There are opportunities now for gels in the City. We can't all do what we want to do.
Amelia No, but we can try. While we're young. Before we're forced to give up.
John She wants to throw herself away!
Amelia She's met a young man, that's all.
John Young man? An artist!
Amelia She tells me he's very clever. He was almost nominated for the Turner prize.
John You see? What did I tell you? Dead animals in formaldehyde. Home videos! Elephant dung!
Amelia (*mildly*) Possibly. He is a sculptor.
John With bits of wire, I suppose? Scrunches up a bicycle wheel and calls it art! Poor old Turner! Huh! Must be turning in his grave!
Amelia Yes, dear, that's very amusing. But now look, you're being very unfair. You haven't even met the young man.
John And I'm not going to.
Amelia You'll have to. She wants to marry him.
John Over my dead body.
Amelia (*after a pause*) Well, I suppose that would solve the problem.
John Oh, no. They won't get a penny from me.
Amelia Yes, John, you've made that very clear. But she's a clever girl. She'll get a job.
John Looking like that?
Amelia Well, not in the City, perhaps.
John Where then? In a circus?

Amelia almost loses patience with him

Amelia Look! We're just going round and around…
John You may be. I know where I stand.
Amelia We'll talk about it this evening—you've got a meeting.

John glances at his watch and reacts

John God, yes. Rosemount. You've made me late.

Amelia double-takes

Ring for Mary, will you?

Amelia does so as John checks he has his glasses, wallet, etc.

Amelia What's Rosemount?
John Just a property company we're taking over.
Amelia That's nice.

Mary, the maid, enters with John's covert coat and bowler

Amelia takes the hat while Mary holds up the coat, for John to shrug into

John As if you were really interested.
Amelia Oh, I am, I am.
John You needn't try to soft-soap me.
Amelia I wouldn't dream of it. (*She fondly places the bowler on his head, at a rakish angle*)

John corrects the hat

John (*better-tempered now*) What are you up to today?
Amelia Saving our starving.

He looks blankly at her

A sub-committee. The officers.
John (*the penny drops*) Oh, that. The charity thing. I'll get out of your way then. (*He moves to kiss her*)
Amelia And I'm not going to let Gerry starve either!

John glares at Mary

Mary bobs and makes a hasty exit

John (*annoyed*) Amelia, she's my daughter!
Amelia Well, I brought her up, you know. She's mine as well.
John It's my responsibility. Leave it to me. I don't want to argue about it. (*He points a warning finger*) And if I find out you're giving her money, I'll cut your allowance as well.

Amelia is quite unfazed

Amelia Yes, dear. (*She kisses him*) Have a good day…

Act I, Scene 1

John Huh!

John goes out

Amelia stays C for a moment, considering, then moves to the other exit

Amelia It's all right. He's gone.

Gerry enters. She is as described, small, mini-skirted, with vividly coloured hair, bedecked with tattoos and pierced jewellery, as weird as you like to make her. She retains her Cheltenham Ladies' College manner, however, having only slightly broadened her vowels to an imitation Cockney

Did you hear all that?
Gerry Most of it.
Amelia (*with more confidence than she feels*) Don't worry. He'll come round.
Gerry Didn't sound like it to me.
Amelia Well ... it may take a little time.
Gerry I haven't got time. We want to go away together. Abroad somewhere perhaps. Now.
Amelia He might be in a better mood tonight. I'll speak to him after dinner.
Gerry It's not as if I need a lot.
Amelia I know...
Gerry But I don't want to give Paul any worries. He needs to concentrate on his work.
Amelia Of course he does.
Gerry He has a marvellous new concept—strange surrealist shapes—he gets them by twisting bicycle wheels...
Amelia Really?
Gerry (*crossly*) Father knows I don't get my trust money until I'm twenty-five. That's why he's behaving the way he does—he's just a bully.
Amelia Darling, he still loves you. And don't worry. I'll see that you get to do whatever you want to do. I don't know how, but I will. Leave it to me.
Gerry Can I? Honestly?
Amelia Honestly.
Gerry You don't think I ought to try and talk to him again?
Amelia Er ... no. If I were you, I'd keep out of his way for the time being. This sort of, er, new persona you've taken on seems to faze him a bit...
Gerry I don't know why. What's wrong with me?
Amelia Nothing, nothing. Now look, darling, I've got a meeting. We'll talk tomorrow. It'll be all right, I promise you.

Gerry throws herself into Amelia's arms

Gerry You're always so good to me. Just like a fairy godmother.
Amelia Stepmother, dear.
Gerry You know what I mean...
Amelia Yes. Off you go... (*She gives Gerry a kiss at the door, and ushers her out*)

Gerry exits

Bye... (*She returns c. She looks out at the audience, sighs deeply*) So many problems!

The Lights fade as Amelia starts to leave the room

Scene 2

Later that morning

Now present with Amelia are the two ladies we saw in the Prologue, Joane Stocks and Rachel Milchan

Amelia is quite angry now, very different from the cool, collected lady we saw in Scene 1

Amelia Agh! It makes me so mad!
Rachel What?
Amelia Everything! The whole world!

Joane has a broad Australian accent and her voice is loud. She—like her husband Ken whom we will see later—tends to employ colourful language. The dialogue in this script just suggests the breadth of their vocabulary, but may be moderately amended

Joane Cheeses you off, don't it?
Amelia I mean, on our last appeal, we raised a quarter of a million pounds.
Joane Too right.
Amelia Have you any idea how much food that buys?
Joane Well, you wouldn't get a ton of caviar.
Amelia No, but if it's wheat or rice, we're talking about acres and acres of warehouse space. Enough to save literally millions of lives.

Rachel's voice is soft, with a hint of native Brooklyn

Rachel Well, I guess that's the idea.

Act I, Scene 2   7

Amelia Oh, that's the idea! But the idea doesn't work. The cost of shipping the food is prohibitive and then, when it does get there, it's nearly all stolen.
Rachel Oh, surely not stolen!
Amelia Oh, I'm sorry, not actually stolen. It's all signed for as being received...
Rachel That's all we can do.
Amelia ...and then it's loaded on to army trucks for distribution. Except for "distribution", read "the black market".
Joane Look, darl, thieving's a way of life out there...
Amelia I've seen the stuff in bazaars—sacks and cartons with our markings still on them—being sold to whoever can afford it, quite blatantly.
Joane Get real, Amelia. That's always going to happen.
Rachel I guess Joane's right. Maybe we should be grateful for what does get through...
Amelia Grateful? After all that time and effort? I mean, we're trying to do something to save the starving, right?
Rachel We're doing what we can.
Amelia Maybe. But it's not enough. Nowhere near enough. We're only scratching at the problem.
Joane OK. We agreed at the meeting, this time we're going to try and raise a million dollars.
Rachel It's not going to be easy. I mean, we're not a big charity.
Joane Rachel's right. I'm amazed we managed to talk those dickheads into it. A lot of them thought we were getting too big for our boots.
Amelia Exactly—because they're little people. They think in terms of local charities, raising enough money to buy a couple of wheelchairs, through jumble sales...
Rachel Is that like a garage sale?
Amelia (*ignoring her*) Or tramps' suppers...
Rachel Why would they invite tramps?
Amelia (*still ignoring her*) They can't grasp the enormity of the situation. They think a million dollars will solve the problem—any problem. But what's a million dollars?

There is a long pause

Joane Is that a question?
Amelia A theoretical one. We three, at least, know a million dollars is small change to some people...

Rachel bridles, immediately sensing this is a reference to her husband

Rachel Well now, listen, it may be to Bill Gates, but it's still a lot of money.

Joane (*almost sadly*) I remember when it used to be. What we would do if we had a million dollars. A fantasy game we played together, like winning the Lottery.
Rachel And I must tell you, Harry has rigid rules about giving to charity. He says you've got to have limits.
Joane Yeh, Ken's a tight-wad too. I tell you, he doesn't often let the moths get out of his wallet, not for charity anyway. If there was a real lot of publicity attached, he might kick in a hundred thousand bucks. Maybe. Of course, if it was for a Government minister, that'd be different—no worries, mate.
Amelia No. Listen to me. I'm not looking for a quick fix. I've already said, even a million dollars won't do what we need to do.
Joane What's that?
Amelia Cut through all that petty thieving in the dockyards. Bribe the soldiers out there ourselves, if we have to, to make sure the food does get through. Or find some ex-SAS tough guys, send them out to do the job.

A pause

Joane Can I pick 'em?
Rachel I'm sure Harry would say that wasn't cost-efficient...
Amelia In relation to a million dollars, you're right. That's what I'm saying. We're not being sufficiently ambitious. We've got to think big.
Joane (*after a pause*) How big?
Amelia Huge.
Joane Oh come on, darl, those wet blankets on the committee would never agree to——
Amelia (*cutting her off*) To hell with the committee. They can't stop us raising money on our own. But we have to do it ourselves. *We* have to. (*She looks at them meaningfully*)

Rachel gets very nervous. Joane buries her face in her hands

Rachel Amelia, now, wait a minute...
Joane Oh, oh. I'm not sure I want to hear this...
Rachel (*brightly*) Maybe we should break for lunch now?
Joane Great idea. I could eat the bum off a low flying duck.
Rachel Did you book San Lorenzo?

Amelia, calm again now, waits for them to finish. Joane shrugs defeat, realizing there will be no budging her

Joane (*sighing*) OK—break it to us gently. What's the crackpot scheme this time? And what are we looking at? (*She jokes*) Two million? Three?

Act I, Scene 2   9

Joane and Rachel exchange smiles at the nonsense of it. Amelia looks from one to the other and allows a pause for impact

Amelia A hundred million.

Long pause

Rachel She's got to be kidding.
Joane I don't think so.
Rachel We have as much chance of making a hundred million dollars——
Amelia (*relentlessly*) Pounds!
Joane —as a pig in… (*She reacts*) Pounds!
Rachel Hey, I agreed to stay on over here so we could really hammer out some kind of meaningful strategy, but——
Joane Look, darl, we don't want to over-feed them, we'd have nothing left to do. (*Hopefully*) You're joking us, right?
Amelia No. And I must say I'm surprised, at both of you. I thought you had more spirit.
Joane Well, we're just colonials, you know? We haven't got that British stiff upper lip.
Rachel Amelia, hey, you must know we have no chance——
Amelia No, I don't! And I'll tell you why not. Just hear me out. Suppose it was not I who was talking, but my husband…?
Rachel (*surprised*) Sir John?
Amelia Yes, Sir John. And suppose he was talking not to you, Rachel, but to your husband…?
Rachel They don't know each other. Not personally.
Amelia …who was listed in Forbes Magazine last year as the twenty-second richest man in America…
Joane Uh, uh, I think I see where this is going…
Amelia And not to you, Joane, but your husband, Kenneth Stocks.
Joane (*grimacing*) The Melbourne Mouth.
Amelia Take-over king, newspaper magnate, brewery mogul…
Rachel And he has television. I saw that magazine article. It says he's——
Joane A bushranger is what it should have said. A bloody highwayman. But go on, make your point.
Amelia My point is that if I were my husband saying to your husbands: "Hey, fellows, how about raising a hundred million quid?"—would they be so shocked?
Rachel Oh, Amelia! They're men!

The other two glare at her

I mean, that's business!

Joane Well, yeh, we are talking about charity—that's a big difference!
Amelia I agree with you. Both of you.
Rachel You do?
Amelia Yes. But my question is, if they can raise that kind of money for business, why can't we raise it for charity—by the same methods?

Joane and Rachel exchange helpless glances. Amelia is irritated by them

I mean, why the hell do we have to have an inferiority complex about this? If they can do it, so can we.
Joane (*shaking her head*) I've lost the plot.
Rachel Amelia, you've obviously got some crazy idea, so you'd better spill it.
Joane I know. We all kill our husbands and when they cark it, we become mega-rich. (*She raises a hand*) I'll barrack for that.
Amelia No. It's a simple business proposition.
Joane I love it.

Amelia picks up the Financial Times *and displays it to them*

Amelia Here's a copy of today's *Financial Times*. Not everybody's favourite reading—but instructive. And one likes to keep up with what one's husband is doing.
Rachel (*shuddering slightly*) I just can't...
Joane (*grimly*) I wish the hell I could.
Amelia Well, I'll tell you—part of the story anyway. (*To Rachel*) Your husband is floating another billion dollar junk issue...

Harry Milchan's obsession with his business is obviously a sore point with Rachel

Rachel Please ... don't tell me...
Amelia Yours just sold a casino in Hong Kong, and an apartment block in Manhattan.
Joane Which one?
Amelia It's on East 72nd.
Joane Oh, that. What's he bought?
Amelia Today? (*She checks the paper*) A string of West End theatres.
Joane Tchah! That bloody actress!
Amelia (*checking further*) Oh—and a stud at Newmarket.
Joane (*thoughtfully*) Now that I could take an interest in.
Amelia Not that kind of stud, darling. Now let's concentrate.
Rachel I'm sorry, I do have to think about my flight back...
Joane Your kid'll survive another day, sweets.

Act I, Scene 2   11

Rachel But I get so nervous when I'm away.
Joane (*ignoring Rachel; to Amelia*) OK. So what's the plan?
Amelia (*to Rachel*) Did you know about Harry's new bond issue?
Rachel Me? No. Well, I suppose so…
Joane I think she means yes.
Rachel Well, I don't take an interest, but I hear Harry on the phone. Even when he's home, he's working…
Amelia Hold it there. (*To Joane*) Did you know about Hong Kong?
Joane (*shrugging*) A bit, I s'pose.
Amelia And Manhattan?
Joane Kind of…
Amelia And the theatres?
Joane Definitely bloody not.
Amelia Or the stud?
Joane He blabbered something about it the other day.
Amelia All right. There's another item here. About my husband. (*She reads*) Sir John Sasson, Chairman of blah blah, blah blah, reported a twenty seven per cent increase in profits, etcetera, etcetera.
Joane Good on you, darls. Hit him for a necklace.
Rachel (*curious*) Did you know?
Amelia Yes, I did. Quite by chance. The Finance Director was here for drinks, with his wife. And she told me.
Joane (*whistling*) No bull?
Amelia Oh, I'm sure she'd never have told anyone else. And I said nothing, of course. But do you see where I'm going?
Rachel No.
Joane I think so—but I hope I'm wrong.
Rachel What do you mean?
Amelia Each one of us was aware of something that only a tiny handful of people knew about—and they were all pledged to secrecy.
Rachel I still don't see what you're getting at…
Joane I think I do.
Amelia (*consulting the paper*) Perth Leisure, the company selling the casino, rose from ten twenty to twelve fifty.
Joane That's definitely worth a necklace.
Amelia (*still reading*) Stocks Real Estate, trading on the New York Stock Exchange, also rose two dollars a share.
Joane And a bracelet. Matching.
Amelia While the shares of that particular company, of which my husband is Chairman, rose by twenty per cent.
Rachel I don't see how all this affects the charity…?
Joane I do. What Amelia is suggesting, in her impeccably well-bred English way, is that we use the good oil…
Rachel The what?

Joane The information...
Amelia ...to make a profitable investment. What could be wrong with that?

Joane is amused but concerned

Joane You know what could be wrong.
Rachel You mean we make money for Save Our Starving by investing? I guess Harry could help with that...
Amelia I know Harry could help.
Rachel Maybe he could devise some kind of bond for us?
Joane Oh, don't be a thick turd, Rachel. Amelia means we use the knowledge we have, or that we obtain...
Amelia ...quite properly, to build a really worthwhile fund.
Rachel (*confused*) You mean our husbands would?
Joane No hubbies, darls. Not with their knowing, anyway. What Lady Amelia is talking about is called "in—sider dea—ling".
Rachel (*shocked*) What?
Joane A crime punishable by death.
Amelia Joane, you do exaggerate.
Joane For guys who get caught, it's a fate worse than death.
Rachel I have heard Harry talk about it...
Joane I bet you have.
Rachel He always laughs...
Joane He's obviously got a great sense of humour. I bet Sir John wouldn't laugh, would he?
Amelia No, you don't understand. Look—we can't be insider dealers because we're not inside. In the sense that we don't work in the city, we're not officially charged with any information whatsoever.
Joane Well, that's true.
Amelia We just happen to pick up odd scraps of information...
Joane (*with a tinkling laugh*) Right. Like the cleaning lady, out of the wastepaper basket.
Amelia Exactly.
Rachel Harry shreds everything, you know.
Joane (*ignoring her*) Except the cleaning lady wouldn't know what to do with it—and if she did, she hasn't got the money.
Rachel Money? This costs money?
Amelia Just a few thousand each, for a start-up fund.
Joane You want to use my bank? Or go offshore?
Rachel (*automatically*) Offshore is best.

Amelia and Joane look at her

That's what Harry says.

Act I, Scene 2					13

Amelia Salzburg. I have it all arranged.
Joane Salzburg? You're not going, are you?
Amelia No. A trusted intermediary.
Joane Who's that?
Amelia I'm not sure yet, but I'll tell you if and when it's agreed. Or you might prefer not to know. It's up to you.
Joane (*admiringly*) You've got this all worked out, haven't you?
Amelia Yes.
Rachel Honey, you do realize you're crazy?
Amelia Am I? Are you saying the scheme won't work?
Joane It's a bloody brilliant idea—if we get the right info.
Amelia That's up to us.
Joane Yeh, but we don't want them to carry the can, do we? I mean I know Stocksie's a bit of a root but I did marry the scumbag.
Rachel Yes, Amelia ... they are our husbands...
Amelia They won't be involved.
Rachel Then that's OK...
Amelia That's the whole point of the scheme. They must never, ever be involved. Then what we're doing would be illegal.
Rachel (*nervously*) Oh?
Joane Yeh, come on, Amelia, there's got to be a catch. Someone's going to lose.
Amelia Who?
Joane I dunno. The owners of the shares we'll be buying?
Amelia Why? Their shares will go up.
Joane Yeh, but whoever buys the shares after. We've been in first, we've had the rich pickings.
Amelia They don't know that. Why should they worry? Someone has to go in first.
Joane It's going to worry some people. The regulation board, for a start.
Amelia At first, they won't even notice. And by the time they do, we'll be out.
Joane I bloody hope so.
Amelia What's a hundred million pounds in terms of the gross trading turnover on the world's stock exchanges? Nothing. A pin prick. A tiny, tiny percentage.

Joane considers, shrugs agreement. Rachel chimes in too

Rachel That's what Harry says.
Amelia Who owns all these shares anyway? Not widows and orphans. Rich corporations. Wealthy individuals.
Joane Just people like us, really.
Amelia Yes. Except we do try to help the poor and starving while they don't

make the slightest effort. Well, if they won't give, we'll take it from them. But painlessly, so it won't even notice.

Joane A bit like Robin Hood?

Amelia If you like. Come on, it's an adventure. So are you both with me?

Rachel Oh, I can't say…

Joane (*unusually sternly*) Do you realize, Amelia, what my husband is going to feel when he finds out someone has bought and sold his stock on inside information? He'll be horrified, shocked, that someone close must have betrayed him—and he doesn't have a clue who it can be! (*She whoops*) Darling, I love it—I'm in!

Rachel I wouldn't want Harry to find out about this.

Joane In your case, if he did, he'd still never believe it.

Amelia It's just passing on a few scraps of information.

Rachel But I wouldn't know if they're important or not.

Amelia Leave that to me.

Joane But how will you know?

Amelia I'll have an adviser.

Joane Who?

Amelia Someone whom no-one—certainly not John—would suspect in a million years. It's——

A knock on the door

Yes?

The door opens and Mary enters

Mary I'm sorry, my lady, I know you said you didn't want to be interrupted…

Amelia That's all right. What is it, Mary?

Mary …but Lord Runcorn is here. He says you're expecting him.

Amelia claps a hand to her forehead

Amelia Oh my God. The charity's patron. I asked him to lunch.

Joane You what?

Amelia I didn't know then what our agenda would be… (*Sweet and calm again*) Show him up, would you, Mary?

Mary bobs and goes out

Rachel We haven't met him, have we?

Amelia I don't know. But watch your language, Joane. It's the Bishop of Walworth.

Act I, Scene 3   15

Joane I'm an atheist. Screw him.
Rachel I'm Jewish.

Amelia, ignoring them both, sweeps majestically past them towards the wings, hand extended in welcome

Amelia (*beaming*) My dear Bishop...

Black-out

Scene 3

The Stocks' apartment in Sydney. Some days later, evening

Ken Stocks, bull-like, fiftyish, is on the phone. Emigrating as a young man from South London, Ken has now become an aggressive Okker, though he still retains a certain rough charm. A bundle of energy, he paces impatiently all the time he is talking. The call lasts as long as necessary to allow Joane time to change into another costume

Ken Yeh... yeh.... Course they'll know someone's buying, but they won't know who or why, will they? They'll just sit on their fat arses and think the stock has suddenly become popular. We'll hit them from every bloody direction, get what we want, and then show our hand.... Right. Right. And then we'll put the boot in, mate. Blast 'em in our newspapers for being stupid dills while we count the loot. (*He continues to stride about as he listens, nodding emphatically as though the other person on the line could see him*) Of course they'll do the same. I know that, you bloody drongo. The difference is they'll have to pay for their advertising and that way I'll take their money twice over.... (*He shakes his head*) No, no, all publicity's good publicity, I don't care what they say about me—I'll start worrying when they stop having a go at me.

Joane enters, her arms full of boxes from expensive London shops

(*Seeing Joane*) Jesus wept! (*Into the phone*) No, I haven't suddenly got religion, my wife's just come in. She doesn't believe it's good for me to be so rich so she tries to help by spending all my money.

Joane ignores him, moves about the room distributing her purchases

Charlie, the only reason I stay in business is to support this sheila.

Otherwise I'd be living on the boat, cruising round Bali. ... (*With a ribald laugh*) Too true, mate, too bloody right I would.

He listens again as Joane opens the boxes, tries out her various purchases, holding them up against herself, pirouetting for effect. She appears to take no notice of Ken whatsoever as he concludes his conversation

Rightyo, let's wind it up. When the market opens Monday, dive in and buy North Star, nothing boomer, right? Just bite-size parcels. And we'll sell as well, taking profit as we go, just to confuse 'em. ... No, dingbat, we'll sell to each other! If we get it right, by Friday we'll have North Star in the bag. ... Nothing can go wrong, mate. At the very worst we greenmail 'em and still get out with a profit—no worries. But listen, sport, keep it under your hat—and keep your hat on tight. Anyone who breaks security on this is going to finish up off Bondi Beach wearin' concrete swimming trunks.

Joane, who has been pretending not to be listening, cannot help reacting to this, but Ken does not see her. He puts down the phone without saying goodbye, then turns and takes in Joane's latest pose

New dress? Where'd you get it?
Joane London. One of them Oxfam shops.
Ken Bloody Chanel, more likely.
Joane Oh, you know all about *haute couture* now, do you? I wonder where you got that from?
Ken Oh, don't start again...
Joane I thought she was an actress, not a model. Or've you got two Barbie dolls in tow now?
Ken D'you want to go out, or what?
Joane Course I bloody do. What'd you think I bought this dress for?
Ken Then stop nagging. (*He starts to move away*)
Joane Well, are you going to put a tie on?
Ken (*turning*) Why? Where are we going?
Joane Somewhere expensive.
Ken Jeez, you're a pain—have you got any idea what it costs me to keep you?
Joane Yep. And you know just how much it would cost to get rid of me. It's cheaper to soldier on, mate—and anyway, what've you got to complain about?

Behind her jibing, there is pain, and Ken knows it, and feels uncomfortable about it. Rather than answer her, he just shrugs in a fed-up manner, starts to leave the room

Ken I'm going to change...

Act I, Scene 3

Joane Ken...

He turns

It's only money.
Ken Yeh. Only money.
Joane Listen, whatever I spend, you hairy dog, it doesn't stop the hurt, you know...?

The underlying sincerity is obvious and it hurts Ken too, but he just growls a reply

Ken Look, if we're going, let's go.
Joane I've just got to phone London.
Ken Uh, huh—the charity thing?
Joane Yeh.
Ken How's it going?
Joane (*after a pause*) On the up and up.
Ken Good.

This brief exchange of civilities encourages Joane to seek to make up for any harsh words

Joane Want me to get you a beer?
Ken Yeh. I'll have a stubbie. (*He starts to leave, then pauses*) I know you don't believe it—but I do love you, Jo.
Joane (*after a pause*) I believe you.
Ken So why do we always——

She interrupts him before he can finish the question, and he knows the answer anyway

Joane You know why, Ken. Because I want you to say "Only you".

There is a moment's awkward silence

Go on... I'll pour your beer.
Ken Yeh.

Joane watches Ken as he goes out somewhat relieved

Joane (*moving to the phone; thoughtfully to herself*) North Star... eh...?

The Lights fade to Black-out

Scene 4

The Milchans' Manhattan penthouse. An evening about a month later

This is where Rachel and Harry live when they're not in Palm Beach

Bonnie, the middle-aged maid (black, perhaps) crosses the stage, pausing to inform Amelia

The following dialogue can be extended as long as necessary to allow Joane to make yet another quick change before entering

Bonnie Mrs Milchan will be right with you, ma'am. Would you and Mrs Stocks like some coffee?
Amelia Not for me, thank you.
Bonnie Or maybe you'd prefer tea. I know you English like tea. I have Earl Grey, I think.
Amelia No, I'm fine. I don't know about Mrs Stocks though. You'll have to ask her when she comes back——

Joane enters

—ah, here she is.
Joane That's one hell of a comfort station Rachel's got...
Amelia I'm sorry?
Joane The dunny... (*She thumbs towards the door*) The loo.
Bonnie Would you like some coffee, ma'am? Or tea?
Joane Maybe something stronger...?
Amelia (*firmly*) Not now, Joane. We're about to start...
Joane I didn't realize this was an AA meeting.
Amelia Thank you, Bonnie.
Bonnie Yes, ma'am... (*She moves to the exit*) Here's Mrs Milchan now.

Bonnie exits as Rachel comes in, breathless

Rachel Sorry I'm late. Benjamin wanted to stay up late to see Poppa when he comes in.
Amelia Poppa? Oh, his father.
Joane Great view of Manhattan, Rachel. Especially from the john. (*To Amelia*) See, I can speak American.
Rachel (*primly*) We say bathroom.
Joane Didn't go for a bath. Went for a...
Amelia (*quickly*) OK, let's hold our meeting. We've a lot to get through and I gather Harry may be back.

Act I, Scene 4   19

Rachel He said he'd be home early.
Joane (*glancing at her watch*) Nine thirty? That's early? (*To Amelia*) OK, what's the score?

They all sit

Amelia (*briskly*) A general review, right?
Rachel I may have to look in on Benjie now and then...
Joane OK... Let's get on with it.
Amelia I'll recap. Our first enterprise was North Star, information donated by Joane, when we were lucky enough to treble our thirty thousand start-up capital.
Joane Fan-tastic!
Amelia Most of which we then played up on John's takeover of Northfields, when we doubled our money.

Joane is enthusiastic. Rachel is hardly listening, her mind on Benjamin

Rachel I'm not sure I shouldn't call the doctor.
Joane For your anxiety neurosis?
Rachel For Benjie—he has a temperature.
Amelia No, dear, I'm sure he's quite well.
Rachel You don't think I ought to?
Amelia No.
Joane Can we get on?
Amelia Then Rachel weighed in with not just one but—(*she checks through her notes*) three, four, five different projects!
Joane Wowee! And Harry didn't suspect. Good on you, Rach.
Rachel (*wistfully*) Harry doesn't think I know anything about anything.
Joane (*with mock astonishment*) Nah!
Amelia You did very well, dear. And we made an absolute killing. So much so, by that time, we had the funds to buy on margin.
Rachel What does that mean?
Amelia Buying shares with money we don't have.
Rachel Isn't that dangerous?
Amelia Yes. But thrilling.
Joane Thrill me—how much did we make?
Amelia Well, believe it or not, we parlayed the two hundred thousand we'd made into nearly two million! And we've only been in business for a month!
Joane I reckon we should do this for a living.
Amelia I haven't finished yet.
Joane There's more?

Rachel There can't be.
Amelia Much more.
Joane Tell me, tell me, tell me...
Amelia Well, we have by now been noticed, of course...
Rachel (*with alarm*) Oh my...
Amelia Not us, personally. I mean the operation that's running in Salzburg.
Joane Trouble?
Amelia No. The point I'm making is that we're now serious punters. Very serious. By which I mean when we move, the market moves.
Joane (*impressed*) Hea-vy!
Amelia Which has begun to cut into our margins.
Rachel By how much?
Amelia Well, in terms of what we want to achieve, it's not the margin that counts for us but what we've grossed at the end of the day.
Joane Yeh—but how much?
Amelia (*glancing at her notes*) You gave us two more big deals in Australia and one in Hong Kong...
Joane Yeah and don't I know about it. Ken's been like a bear with a sore doodah.
Amelia That's what I mean. People are beginning to notice.
Joane Too bad! Is it worth it?
Amelia To us, definitely. Our little plunge on those three deals netted us over ten million!
Joane What?! That's terrific!
Amelia Which we doubled again...
Rachel No!
Amelia Oh yes—when one of John's companies bought a chain of stores in the United States.
Joane Far out!
Amelia And he was very unhappy, I can tell you.
Rachel (*thinking*) You know, Harry hasn't been himself at all lately.
Amelia I'm not surprised.
Joane I'm knocked out. Hey Rach, how did you manage to get all this info?
Rachel He keeps it on a computer in his study.
Joane And you know how to get into it?
Rachel Oh, sure. I majored in computer studies at Columbia.
Joane (*with respect*) Wow!
Rachel What did you do before you got married?
Joane I was, er, a hostess...
Rachel (*innocently*) No, I mean before you got married...?
Amelia (*quickly changing the subject*) So would you ladies like to know what our activities on behalf of Save Our Starving have raised in total?
Joane You bet!

Act I, Scene 4   21

Rachel (*half rising*) If I could just check on Benjie first...?
Joane Oh Jeez, let 'im play with his willy.
Amelia We're almost through.

Rachel subsides

> The grand total, ladies, is twenty million, three hundred and seventy-three thousand, four hundred and sixty-five English pounds...

Joane and Rachel gasp. Amelia holds up a hand

> Which goes up every minute as we speak, because, naturally, it's deposited on high-interest, short-term money market rates.

Rachel But don't we have to take it out when we make our investments?
Amelia Absolutely not. We bet on account and, since we never lose, we never have to pay out. I can tell you, the bank manager's very, very pleased with us.
Joane Cripes, so he should be! We're a money-making machine.
Amelia (*adopting an Aussie accent*) Over forty million Australian dollars, darlsy.
Rachel At this rate, we must be almost there?
Joane Dam' right.
Amelia If we had two more deals which doubled our money, we would be. But we may have to settle for twenty-thirty per cent profit margins from now on, so it might take us another five or six.

Joane makes a face of disappointment

Joane Yeh, right. An' security's gettin' tighter all the time. I practically have to wait for Ken to talk in his sleep. And most of what he says is bloody nauseating. But I'll do my bit. How long you in New York for, Amelia? Wanna come shoppin' tomorrow?
Amelia I'd love to, darling, but I can't. I came over today with John for a board meeting—the company he's just bought—and we're getting Concorde back, first thing.
Joane OK. Suppose it's no use askin' you, Rach?
Rachel Not tomorrow. I think I'll have to keep Benjie home from school.
Joane No worries. Keep up the computer studies, darl.
Rachel Eh? Oh, yes. I shall have to be careful, of course. Harry hasn't said anything to me directly but I know how worried he is.
Amelia They're all worried—but it'll be over soon. We'll get out, just like we said we would, and then we'll be able to channel our energies into making that money work. We can personally supervise the operations, to

make sure no-one pulls the wool over our eyes, and the food does get through.

Rachel Well, I don't think I'll be able to get out to Africa. I have Benjie, you see, and Harry——

Joane Forget it. Anyway, it's not your style, Rach, banging heads together. We love it. What d'you say, Mel?

Amelia (*briskly*) I can't wait to see that first plane loaded.

There is a sound of an elevator's ping from the adjacent hallway

Harry (*off*) Hi, honey...

Joane (*in an American accent*) ...I shrunk the kids.

Harry Milchan enters. He is a middle-aged, nervous-mannered, totally preoccupied, nondescript Jewish businessman

Hey, sweetie... (*He stops and blinks as he sees the others*) Oh, sorry ... you're in a meeting.

Rachel No, honey. We're all through now. I don't think you've met my friends. Lady Amelia Sasson—she's from England.

Harry (*shaking hands*) Sir John's wife?

Amelia That's right.

Harry (*always business-blinkered*) Just took over Q & B. Bad business.

Amelia He thinks it's a very good business.

Harry Oh, I don't mean Q & B. But there was some insider dealing there... (*He flutters his hands*) I guess you wouldn't understand.

Amelia I'm afraid I don't. (*She bats her eyelashes*) And if I did, I know I couldn't talk about it.

Harry (*apologetically*) Of course not...

Rachel (*leading him to Joane*) And Joane Stocks, from Australia.

Harry Ken Stocks' wife?

Joane Yeh. G'day. How're you going?

Harry Fine, thanks.

They shake hands

Ken Stock's wife, huh? That's a coincidence.

Joane No. We meant it—at the time.

Harry I mean ... no, I was thinking of something else. Nice to meet you ladies. Don't let me interrupt.

Amelia No, we were just leaving...

He gestures protest

Act I, Scene 4

Really...
Joane (*taking her cue*) Yeh, we're off. See you, darls.

Joane kisses Rachel while Amelia shakes hands with Harry

Amelia Goodbye. Rachel...

Amelia kisses Rachel as Joane waves goodbye to Harry

Rachel sees Amelia and Joane out to the elevator in the hall, leaving Harry pondering. Then Rachel returns

Rachel I'm glad you're back, Harry. Benjie's been asking for you.
Harry Er, yeh. I'm still working, honey. I just wanted to get away from the office.
Rachel Well, OK, but go up and see Benjie first. Then I'll bring some coffee to your den.
Harry Fine. Er—maybe, no... I think I'll fix myself a drink.
Rachel A drink? You mean alcohol?

He nods

Harry, you never drink. Except at weekends.
Harry Well, I kind of feel like one. I've just got to relax, honey...
Rachel Well, sure... I wish there was something I could do to help. (*She moves to caress him*) Here, take your jacket off, sit down now... (*She eases him into a comfortable chair, starts to massage him*) Gosh, you're so tight!
Harry I know, I know. I feel kind of—bunched up inside.
Rachel That's it. You're really tense. What is it, honey? Business troubles?
Harry (*sighing deeply*) Big, big troubles.
Rachel Is it some kind of a deal you've got a problem with? I mean, I know I don't understand, but you ought to try talking about it... I can just sense everything, you know, bottled up inside you...
Harry You're right. Believe me, you're right. I wish there was someone I could talk to. You know what I mean when I say that, honey...
Rachel (*massaging, soothing him*) Sure...
Harry What I'm trying to say is, I don't know who I can trust, not any more. I thought I had the loyalty of everyone in that office. Everyone! I ought to have, I pay them enough. But some people are so greedy. All they want to do is to make money. Can you believe that, Rachel?
Rachel (*rather sadly*) I believe it. (*She continues to massage him*)
Harry They've betrayed me, Rachel.
Rachel Who's betrayed you, sweetheart?

Harry That's what I don't know. That's what I've got to find out. I've done everything. Changed all the entry codes on all the computers. Had the offices de-bugged, all of 'em, swept clean from top to bottom.

Rachel Gee, Harry, what is it? Is it the Legionnaires' disease? They say it starts in the water tanks. Oh my God! Maybe that's what's wrong with Benjie...!

Harry Rachel, please! I don't mean defumigation or sterilization. I'm talking about electronic sweeping. I'm talking about treachery. I'm talking about investigation—by the SEC!

Rachel (*slowly, as the importance sinks in*) The Securities and Exchange Commission.

Harry Right! Give me Legionnaires' disease any time...

Rachel (*automatically*) Harry, don't say that.

Harry Legionnaires ... do me a favour. But an investigation by the SEC... It's what I've worried about all my life. It's the only thing that gives me nightmares. I wake up sweating sometimes, crying out "It wasn't me, I didn't do it".

Rachel embraces him comfortingly

Rachel Honey, baby...

Harry And I know I'm lying. But this time I'm not. I've done nothing. I've told no-one. And yet it still leaks out. It's as if someone could read inside my head. It's like there's a ghost walking around. It's spooky!

Rachel resumes the massage, so that she can stand behind Harry and he does not see her reaction. She is troubled by the effect that this is obviously having on her husband

Rachel You'd better tell me exactly what's happened, Harry. Come on...

Harry OK. Exactly, I don't know. But I do deals, right? I put out bond issues and sometimes we use the bond to take over a business maybe. Something not doing so well but with a lot of assets we can break up, sell off cheap, make a fast buck.

Rachel What about the people and their jobs? I mean, in the recession——

Harry (*interrupting impatiently*) We're not talking about people, we're talking about money, right? A lot of money, a *lot* of money. So if someone finds out what we're doing, they know we've done our homework, right? They know this is big bucks and they want to be in on it, OK?

Rachel (*helpfully*) You could sell them some of your bond...

Harry The bond is sold. Everyone's committed. (*He holds a hand under his chin*) Up to here! OK, they know the business must be worth twice what it's quoted on Wall Street or wherever, so they buy in, right?

Act I, Scene 4 25

Rachel Right. And the price goes up I do understand, Harry. That's good—if you've just bought the company.

Harry (*gritting his teeth*) We haven't bought it yet—that's the problem! Some snake knows what we're doing and has bought in ahead of us. We've lost our edge.

Rachel Gosh! (*She pauses*) Edge?

Harry (*not really listening*) OK, we're still in a greenmail situation. Maybe we can avoid taking a bath. Even make a profit, selling them back their own shares. But it's all gone sticky and the SEC wants to know what's going on here...

Rachel But why should the SEC blame you, Harry?

Harry Good question. In fact it's *the* question, Rachel. OK, I've made a few million dollars, maybe a billion even, but it was all business. Why do they always suspect me?

Rachel Do they?

Harry Do they investigate Morgan? Or Grenfell? Or Sachs? Or Goldman? Why do they have to think I'm involved just because someone makes a fast buck?

Rachel I guess it's because you're so good at making money for people, sweetheart...

Harry Right! All I do is make millions of people happy and, suddenly, that's a crime! What's so terrible?

Rachel (*reasonably*) Well, there must be something—specific—that's worrying them.

Harry Oh, there is, there is. Sure, information leaks. And also people guess right. And there's some good guessers around, believe me.

Rachel Well, that's no crime.

Harry No, sir! But you see, Rachel, sometimes—and I know, honey, you'll find it hard to believe these things happen—sometimes it's because certain parties connive to cash in on the knowledge they have that these things are about to happen...

Rachel (*shocked*) Oh, no! That's terrible!

Harry It's the most terrible thing that can happen if you're in the financial services sector—well it is, if you're caught at it. It's called "insider dealing".

Rachel Insider what, dear?

Harry Dealing! Dealing! (*In his agitation, he has to get up, starts walking around*) And it's happened to me—I mean, deals I've been associated with—what I'm saying is, I'm a victim!

Rachel Oh, Harry! I never knew.

Harry More than once. But once in a while, you can live with it. Twice becomes a problem. Three times in a short while, you change all the locks and fire everyone whose life doesn't depend on your existence—even them, unless you need them. But four times when the finger is pointing at you, boom, the SEC are in there, baby...!

Rachel Oh, gosh! You make it sound awful.

Harry Don't use nice words like "awful", Rachel. This is the SEC we're talking about. It's like the police, the Revenue, the Drugs Enforcement Agency.

Rachel That bad?

Harry Worse. Much worse. It's like the old Russian KGB and Israel's Mossad rolled into one. I mean, don't talk to me about the Gestapo—they were pussy-cats compared with these people.

Rachel This is terrible.

Harry No, it's not terrible, Rachel. You have to improve your vocabulary, honey, this is on a different plane from terrible. It's disastrous. It's catastrophic. No, these words understate the position. It's apocalyptic.

Rachel Oh. (*She pauses*) It's really bad, then?

Harry throws up his arms

I'm sorry, honey, I don't know what that word means.

Harry, momentarily guilt-stricken, moves to embrace her

Harry That's OK, sweety-pie. I don't either. But we both saw the movie, right? It means: like hell!

Rachel Oh yeh. (*She pauses*) Four times, did you say?

Harry Huh! Four, they've already raised their ugly heads. Five, they issue garrottes to all personnel. And it's happened to me five times! In two months! Five times someone has played the market and I am the object of their suspicions. Me? As if I'd be such a schmuck! To risk my life, my business; my wife, my baby... (*He pauses, tears in his eyes*)

Rachel In that order?

But Harry is not listening. He is pacing furiously, talking to himself

Harry Me! Once, yes, OK, let's take a chance. Twice, well, hell, we got away with it before, let's party ... but five times! What do they think, I'm meshuggah? (*He gestures the question wildly to Rachel*)

Rachel You're just overwrought.

Harry is astounded

Harry Rachel, I love you dearly, but you have a kind of maddening way of always totally understating what is happening in the world, unless it concerns Benjie, when you kind of go into reverse.

Act I, Scene 4

Rachel (*vindicated*) See?
Harry I am not overwrought. I am a mass of tangled, seething emotions. What you see before you is a human time bomb, which is going to detonate at any moment.
Rachel (*comforting*) I'll get Bonnie to make some decaff. (*She moves towards Harry, strokes his back again*)

Harry is broken for the moment. There is obviously nothing to be gained from expounding his woes to Rachel. He needs to be alone now, to work this thing out

Harry I must work on the computer. I'll be in the den.

She nods and starts to move away

I won't take any calls. Put on the machine or if you answer, say I'm not here. You don't know where I am. Trust no-one.

She nods and starts to go but Harry stops her again

Don't let anyone in. Don't even answer if anyone calls up from the lobby. And don't wait up for me. I may work all night. You understand, sweetheart?
Rachel Sure I do, Harry. OK, I won't wait up. But you must go and see Benjie first.
Harry Benjie? (*A paranoiac thought strikes him*) Has Benjie been playing with my computer?
Rachel Of course not, honey, he's got his own. But he has a fever, Harry. And he wants to see Poppa.
Harry (*holding on to his temper*) Rachel, you do understand everything I've been saying to you?
Rachel Yes, dear.
Harry That I am the subject of a Securities Exchange Commission investigation?

She nods

And you want me to go up and kid around with Benjie?
Rachel Yes, I do.
Harry Right now?
Rachel Right now.

Harry takes a deep gulp of breath, recognizes he will have no peace until he does what she wants. *He shakes his head in total wonder at this attitude but does not make a fuss, just holds up his hands in surrender and leaves the room*

Rachel watches him go, then turns back to face the audience, as she ponders over their conversation and everything that has been happening as the result of the syndicate's activities

(*Eventually*) Wow!

Black-out

Scene 5

The Belgravia drawing-room. A morning some weeks later

Amelia is speaking on the phone. Joane sits sprawled in an armchair nearby, listening

Amelia Yes.... Yes... I understand.... No.... No.... Don't... just, er, stay cool—I'll talk to Joane.... OK.... Right.... Bye, Rachel—oh, is he? Dear Benjie... (*She glances at Joane*)

Joane makes a face

Give him a kiss for me. And for Joane.

Joane winces

Bye... (*She puts the phone down*) Rachel's husband is very nervous.
Joane Hah! So's mine!
Amelia Apparently Harry Milchan is being investigated by the Securities and Exchange Commission.
Joane So's Stocksy.
Amelia Ken? You didn't tell me that.
Joane Agh, they're always investigating him. How d'you think he got rich? Wasn't through being a salvo.
Amelia (*troubled*) Oh, dear.
Joane No worries—Ken's always at least one step ahead of 'em.
Amelia Except in this case, he doesn't know what he's one step ahead of— he's not the offending party.
Joane Too true. That's why he's so rat-arsed about it. I tell you, it's funny.
Amelia Funny?

Act I, Scene 5

Joane Yeh, seein' him chargin' around like a Mallee bull, suspecting all his best mates.
Amelia Oh. That's rather sad, isn't it?
Joane You don't know his mates. They're all as bent as he is, or try to be. That's what's funny. For years, all of 'em have been scamming the markets—it's well known but no-one's ever been able to prove it. Ken was way too smart for that. Now they're really breathing down his neck, determined to get him, and he doesn't even know what for! I'm telling you, he's scared out of his pants. If he was guilty, he'd know how to duck and dive—it's being not guilty that's blowing his brains. What brains he's got left. (*With some fondness*) Stupid old dag.
Amelia What's a dag?
Joane (*shrugging*) Just a sheep turd ... but matted, you know?
Amelia (*faintly*) Er, yes. Anyway, you can imagine how John feels—though for quite different reasons. As Chairman of the Stock Exchange, he's obliged to be a pillar of respectability—and he is. To a degree, I must tell you, that is sometimes asphyxiating!
Joane (*not at all sure what that means*) Yeh, well...
Amelia As soon as the various watchdog institutions got on to him, he was baying for blood, heads had to roll—the poor lamb never realized of course that his firm was a prime suspect. Made me feel quite guilty.
Joane It's Rafferty's rules...

Amelia decides not even to ask what she means

Amelia So things are very, very tense right now.
Joane For all of us.
Amelia Especially Rachel.
Joane Poor cow.
Amelia Er, yes, I think she is the most vulnerable.
Joane You think maybe we should call it a day, uh? Spit the dummy?
Amelia I don't know. Yes, of course I'd like to call a halt straight away but even if we did stop, the investigating authorities wouldn't. I understand the SEC have people over here right now, sniffing around.
Joane Let's stop it, then. It was a great lurk you thought up, darl, but—well, it's all beginning to go over the top.
Amelia But it's so frustrating. Everything's worked like a dream till now. Couldn't believe my eyes when I checked the market prices this morning. We have so many deals going, I forget about some of them. But we've got more than fifty million in the bank now—we're half way there!
Joane You've got nerves of steel, Amelia. I'd have got out fast, shot through like a Bondi tram...
Amelia You're right. Perhaps we did overplay our hand. It's just that that kind of money...

Joane Gives you a rush. Right. But it's not our money.
Amelia That's true. And we owe it to the charity now to realize our holdings as quickly as possible and start using the cash. Just in case anyone did get on to us and seek to freeze our assets.
Joane They couldn't do that, could they?
Amelia I don't know, but I don't want to take any chances. It's the charity's money, as you said, that's sitting there in Salzburg, and we can't risk it. So we'll suspend trading—I think that's the phrase—as of now, if you agree?
Joane I'm in. What about Rach? Will she be all right?
Amelia I'm sure she'll be delighted. And if the worse does come to the worst...
Joane See you in Cell Block H.
Amelia I don't think so. So long as we have transferred the money to Save Our Starving, no-one's going to demand it back.
Joane That's good thinking, Batman. Hell, they're not going to put the Bishop in jail.
Amelia And even John's not going to want a scandal.
Joane Dam' right. You've convinced me. Let's do it.
Amelia (*moving towards the phone*) I'll call Salzburg, give the orders now. (*She lifts the receiver and dials. Into the phone*) Oh, hallo, the Director please.... Mata Hari. (*She cups the receiver. To Joane*) My code name.... (*Into the phone*) Yes? ... Back in five minutes? ... Will you call me then? ... Thank you. Hari, yes, H-A-R-I. Goodbye. (*She puts the phone down and pauses, suddenly irresolute*) Joane, we are doing the right thing, aren't we?
Joane (*shrugging*) The heat's on. We've got to bail out. Or they'll latch on to us for sure. It's gone too far.
Amelia Oh God... (*She bites her lip, moves away from the phone*) Divorces might be in order...
Joane Not for me.
Amelia No?
Joane No. Ken'd have me garrotted in some King's Cross alley.
Amelia You are joking?
Joane It wouldn't be the first time he'd threatened it.
Amelia (*appalled*) Why?
Joane (*shrugging*) Cheaper than a divorce.
Amelia You've talked about it then? Divorce?
Joane Every time he leans up against another bimbo.
Amelia Is that often?

Joane shrugs

That must be awful for you.

Act I, Scene 5

Joane I've lived with it for so long, I—I was going to say, I've got used to it, but that's not true—I never could.
Amelia (*tentatively*) Did you ever...?
Joane Not till recently—though I had plenty of offers. But I don't know, I just loved the old sod and I couldn't fancy anyone else. Then, one day, I looked around and saw what all my mates were doing and thought: why not? "Get yourself a toyboy, Joane". So I did.
Amelia (*shockingly thrilled*) No!
Joane Ken'd go mad if he knew—men are like that, aren't they? Funny thing is, I don't crack at him half as much as I used to, so he kind of gets the benefit of Carlo too, don't he?
Amelia Carlo?
Joane (*with enthusiasm*) He's be-udiful! Like an Aussi Sylvester Stallone—but tall with it. And a lot younger. In fact, ten years younger than I am but—and you'll never believe this, I find it hard to believe myself—he really loves me. He says so, anyway. He's on at me all the time to leave Stocksy.
Amelia (*tactfully*) Are you sure he's not...?
Joane After my money? A fat divorce settlement? Who cares? I've thought about it, naturally, but he swears he isn't...
Amelia He would, wouldn't he?
Joane Yeh, but he's got money himself. Or his people have. A lot.
Amelia What does he do?
Joane (*vaguely*) Works in some kind of family business. No, I've seen where they live, and how—they're rich.
Amelia (*uncertainly*) Well, that's—wonderful. But do you love him?
Joane Hell, I don't know. He excites me more than Ken ever could, and he's kind and good-mannered—a really well brought up boy—he makes Ken look such a toad. Which he is, anyway.
Amelia Then what are you waiting for?
Joane (*sincerely*) I want to know it's for real. (*She shrugs*) As for leaving Ken, the only thing that puzzles me is why I even have to think about it...
Amelia You've been together for a long time.
Joane Yeh, and we've been through a lot together. We were just kids when we met. I was a banana bender. Y'know? Down from Queensland. I went to Sydney and got a job as a hostess in a club at the Cross. Ken was an electrician, just off the boat—he came from London—and full of himself, dead lairy. (*She smiles at the memory*) Unstoppable. Anyway, one night a couple of larrikins gave me a bit of a hassle, Stocksy laid 'em out flat, both of them. It was love at first sight. He had so much go in him, you know? Made you feel breathless just to be with him. So we shacked up together for a while and then——

There is a knock at the door

Amelia Yes? (*To Joane, remembering*) I must make that call, they haven't rung me back.

Mary enters

Mary Sorry to interrupt you, my lady. There's a Miz Wallis to see you.

Amelia frowns, the name means nothing

She doesn't have an appointment, but she says it's important—about the charity. And as you were having a sub-committee meeting, I thought...

Amelia shrugs towards Joane, begging pardon for the interruption. Joane shrugs back

Amelia Yes, all right, we might as well see her... (*To Joane*) Sorry...
Mary Yes, my lady ... oh, her card.

Mary moves to hand a visiting card to Amelia before leaving the room

Amelia glances at it

Amelia D L Wallis...? (*She suddenly freezes as she reads on*) Oh God!
Joane (*alarmed*) Amelia ... what is it?
Amelia (*reading*) "Investigator, Securities and Exchange Commission"!
Joane Oh, jeez. Just when we thought we were home and hosed. The SEC? Here? Now?
Amelia Now!

The phone rings

Oh damn! It's Salzburg!

They look at each other in frozen horror. Then someone knocks on the door. It is like the rap of doom. And, as the phone continues to ring piercingly—

—*the* Curtain *falls*

ACT II

Scene 1

The Belgravia drawing-room. Morning, continuing from the end of Act I

As the Curtain *rises, Wallis strides across to Amelia and puts out a hand. She is a rather butch-looking lady of indeterminate age, 40-50 perhaps, of stocky build. She wears a severely cut business suit and has a severe manner to match. This is undoubtedly a tough cookie*

Amelia, Joane and Mary are in the same position as before. Amelia is still holding the card

The phone is still ringing

Wallis Lady Sasson. How're you doing? D'you want to answer that?
Amelia (*shaking Wallis's hand*) Mary, would you…?

Mary goes immediately to answer the phone. Wallis glances around during the following

Mary Hallo… (*She cups the phone*) It's for a Mrs Hari, my lady.
Amelia One of the ladies of the committee. Say she's not here, will you.
Mary (*into the phone*) Sorry, she's not here. … Thank you. (*She puts down the phone*)
Amelia Thank you, Mary.

Mary bobs and goes out

(*To Wallis*) I'm so sorry, you were saying?
Wallis How're you doing?
Amelia I'm doing quite well, thank you, but I'm sure there must be some mistake. Perhaps it's my husband you want to see?
Wallis Maybe. Maybe not. But right now, it's you I want to talk to. (*She looks meaningfully towards Joane*) You and your friend.
Joane (*weakly*) G'day.
Wallis (*moving towards her*) Mrs Stocks, I guess? (*She extends her hand*) How're you doing?

Joane Hi.

They shake hands. There is a moment of silence as Wallis moves around the room, appreciating it. Then she looks again at Amelia and Joane, who stand waiting guiltily

Wallis (*briskly*) OK, let's cut the crap. Some hitherto unknown company based in Salzburg has been taking the markets for a big ride, trading on what is obviously inside information.

Amelia has recovered her self-assurance now. She looks politely concerned

Amelia Salzburg?
Wallis You know it?
Amelia Didn't Mozart live there?
Wallis (*crisply*) Mozart, schmozart.
Amelia I don't know Schmozart.
Wallis As soon as we guessed what was happening, we started to track all unusual stock movements, and then analysed them. And what d'you think?
Amelia I can't imagine.
Wallis OK? I'll tell you. We found that every one of those market moves was connected with a company controlled by one of three sources, whether they were buying or selling. Do you follow me?
Amelia With great difficulty.
Wallis OK, I'll make it simple for you by naming the three sources, whereby you will understand the purpose of this call. They were, basically, companies controlled by your husband, Sir John Sasson...
Amelia Oh, really? Well, my husband does buy and sell companies...
Wallis (*to Joane*) ...Your husband, Kenneth Stocks...
Joane (*feigning astonishment*) Nah...?
Wallis And an operator in the United States, one Harry Milchan...
Amelia I'm afraid I've never heard of him.
Wallis Strange, since his wife seems to be a friend of yours.
Amelia (*wide-eyed*) Oh, you mean Rachel! (*To Joane*) Did you know she was married to a man called—what was his name again?
Joane I thought her husband was called Herschel.
Amelia Or was it Lew? Surely it was Lew?
Wallis Ladies, I ask you again, with great respect, to cut the crap. You do know Harry Milchan. You have met him at their penthouse apartment on one-two-six East Fifty-Seventh Street. I doubt you ever knew him as Herschel or even Lew. I have a full record of your movements over the last several weeks.
Joane (*angrily*) Hell, you mean you've been following us?

Act II, Scene 1   35

Amelia Surely we have a privacy law?
Wallis No, you don't have a privacy law and yes, you have been under surveillance. (*To Joane*) Your movements, Mrs Stocks, were of particular interest but— (*she flips open a notebook*) we'll stick to the three of you. (*She reads*) Lunch at La Cirque in New York ... a dinner in London at Le Gavroche... (*She shakes her head*) You guys know how to eat well...
Amelia This is intolerable.
Wallis Then don't tolerate it. If you want to try suing the SEC, go right ahead but, if I were you, I'd ask your husband first.

Amelia stops protesting. She exchanges troubled glances with Joane as Wallis takes another, studied walk around the room

> How the rich live, uh? But listen, I got to hand it to you, this was a tough assignment. I guess that's why I got it. I'm a top operator but I got a low profile, you know what I mean?

Joane You mean, like a snake?
Wallis (*ignoring Joane; to Amelia*) No-one suspects me. I don't look like an investigator, right?
Amelia Well... Miss Marple, perhaps?
Wallis Never heard of her. But I get in places other people don't. I can figure out what other people can't... (*She puts a finger to the side of her nose, knowingly*) Like that whole Salzburg operation?

Amelia decides to make a fight of it

Amelia Entirely legitimate, surely?
Wallis Oh yeh ... someone there was just buying and selling shares—no harm in that. But someone was telling them what to buy and sell, and those are the parties that I find of considerable interest.
Amelia You don't imagine I was involved?
Wallis I didn't. Not till I got a print-out of your telephone calls to Salzburg. And even then, it could have been Sir John.
Amelia (*sharply*) That's ridiculous.
Wallis I agree. He's got too much to lose. But who then, and why?
Joane (*after a pause*) You're going to tell us, right?
Wallis Dam' right I am. I enquired and found Sir John had no known connections with Stocks or Milchan—and that threw us for quite a while— but then... (*She pauses for dramatic effect*) I was reading a magazine in a *salon de coiffeurs*...
Amelia A what?
Joane A barber's shop.
Amelia Oh. (*She studies Wallis's close crop*) You must let me know the name of your hairdresser...

Joane So we know not to go there...
Wallis (*bulldozing on*) One of them society magazines. And then I saw it. The men weren't connected. But their wives were.
Amelia We're all officers of SOS, the Save Our Starving Campaign. What of it?
Wallis That's just what I asked myself. What of it? So I checked around some more. And I found the charity has had some pretty substantial hand-outs recently, all anonymous. (*She glowers at Amelia during the following*)
Amelia (*imperiously*) You are not seriously accusing a major international charity—among whose patrons are numbered the Bishop of Walworth and Hillary Clinton—of carrying out some kind of clandestine insider trading—is that what you call it?
Wallis I sure as hell am calling it that and I just told you, I don't know if the charity is involved. But if it is, and I can prove it, I'll put Mrs Clinton in the dock and the Bishop of Walworth. But I think it's you.

Joane and Amelia reply almost as one

Joane Me?
Amelia Me?
Wallis Yes, and yes, and if you'd like to ask a proxy question on behalf of your friend Mrs Milchan, yes again.
Amelia Preposterous. Why would we do that?
Wallis That's what I thought you might like to tell me.
Joane What are you, some kind of nong? We ain't poor, you know?
Wallis I do know.
Amelia So what motive could we possibly have?
Wallis How about the charity? (*She looks from one to the other in the long silence that ensues*) I thought so.
Amelia (*quickly*) That's absolute nonsense. But—just for the sake of argument—suppose it was?
Wallis OK.
Amelia It really wouldn't be good publicity for the SEC, would it, to steal a hundred million dollars from starving children?
Wallis (*whistling*) Wow! Is that how much you've made?
Amelia (*right on top of her, realizing her mistake*) I meant for the sake of argument.
Wallis OK. I'll answer that. We love bad publicity. We like nothing more than to be pictured as some kind of reincarnation of the Spanish Inquisition. When it happens—and it does—it doubles our revenues.
Joane (*suddenly fed up*) OK, Torquemada, quit twisting the thumbscrews. Are you going to arrest us or not?
Wallis (*after a pause*) Not.

Act II, Scene 1 37

Amelia (*amazed*) Not? Why not?
Joane (*shrewdly*) Because I suspect Miz Wallis has something else in mind.
Wallis Correct.
Amelia (*lost*) I don't understand.
Wallis OK. I'll explain. You ladies hit upon a scheme which was not only ingenious, but unique. Because only you three could, in a short time, have drawn upon such exclusive sources of information—and never even have been suspected. No-one, in my experience, has ever made so much money in so short a time, not playing the markets anyway—except maybe George Soros. And if you'd known when to stop, I guess we'd never have found out.
Amelia (*quickly*) We have stopped.
Wallis No, you haven't.
Amelia Well, we're going to.
Wallis No, you're not.
Joane You just don't get it, do you, Amelia?
Wallis What I am saying, in a nutshell, is that in all my years of delving into the murky depths of international high finance, this is the most diabolically clever get-rich-quick scheme I have ever encountered...
Amelia And?
Wallis And I want a part of it.
Joane It's a hook. I saw it coming, all the way.
Amelia (*genuinely aghast*) But we couldn't possibly...
Wallis You couldn't? Think of the alternative, Lady Sasson. And you wouldn't find my demands excessive...
Joane Just the odd ten million or so...
Wallis Exactly. Think of it as an insurance policy...
Joane ...Or protection money.
Wallis What's so terrible? (*A trifle wistfully*) Is it so wrong for me to want to be like you?
Joane Oh... come to lunch.
Wallis (*keenly*) Really?
Joane No, not really!
Amelia No, look, we just couldn't. The answer must be no.
Wallis Think about it. You'll soon change your mind.
Joane How long've we got?
Wallis You're lucky. I have to get back to New York.
Joane (*grimly*) So have we.
Wallis Good. You can consult with your fellow conspirator. Make up your minds before the end of the week.
Amelia (*appalled*) That's only five days!
Wallis I'll be back in London next Monday— (*with a curiously formal little bow*) when I will call on you again, if I may?

Amelia (*automatically polite*) Oh, please do…
Joane (*harshly*) Creep!

Wallis confronts them both. There is no mistaking the threat in her tone

Wallis Just be ready. That's all.

Black-out

Scene 2

The Milchans' New York apartment. Morning, two days later

Rachel is walking about the room distractedly. Amelia watches her

Rachel This is just awful. I got to tell you. When you called, I lay awake all night, thinking about it and I lost my nerve—completely. Then today—I'm sorry—I just had to call Harry.
Amelia Oh my God. What did he say?
Rachel I haven't been able to speak to him. He's not taking calls.
Amelia Well, thank goodness…
Rachel I even went to his office but they told me I had to make an appointment—with my own husband. And anyway, Harry wasn't taking meetings any more. Oh gosh! He is so churned up about this.
Amelia I must admit, I thought about confessing to John…
Rachel And?
Amelia I didn't think about it for very long.
Rachel What about Joane?
Amelia Oh, I don't think she ever considered telling Ken.
Rachel No?
Amelia No. He'd probably have arranged for her to get beaten up. That man's an absolute thug.
Rachel Oh well, that's good. I mean, good she didn't call him.
Amelia Yes. But she did call Carlo.
Rachel Who's Carlo?
Amelia Her boyfriend. He's here in New York.
Rachel (*after a pause*) But Joane's married.
Amelia Rachel, that's not relevant just now.
Rachel She didn't tell him, did she?
Amelia Unfortunately, yes.
Rachel Everything?
Amelia She says not. Just outlined the problem, she says.

Act II, Scene 2   39

The intercom rings. Rachel answers it

Rachel Hallo? ... Oh, right. Yes, we're expecting her. (*She replaces the receiver*) Security. It's Joane. (*She resumes their conversation*) Why did she call him?
Amelia (*shrugging*) To ask his advice, I suppose.
Rachel About what?
Amelia I suppose this American woman who's trying to blackmail us.
Rachel You mean the SEC investigator?
Amelia (*studying the visiting card*) D L Wallis, as it says on her card. Sexless, isn't it? But then so's she.
Rachel I don't understand how this Carlo could help.
Amelia Nor do I.

We hear the sound of a ping from the hallway

Rachel That's the elevator.

Rachel goes out to the hall

Amelia shakes her head and stares out of the window

Rachel enters with Joane

Joane Sorry I'm late.
Amelia This is an important meeting, Joane.
Joane I was with Carlo.
Amelia That's no surprise.
Rachel (*reproachfully*) Joane, you know you really shouldn't...

Joane and Amelia turn to glare at her. She shuts up

Joane (*defiantly*) He wanted me to meet his uncle on Long Island.
Amelia Joane, could we leave your social life out of this, just for a moment?
Joane But he has a lot of influence in financial circles here, Carlo says. And he knows this D L Wallis.
Amelia Oh my God. You didn't tell him the whole story?
Joane (*defensively*) Well, not everything, no. But he says he might be able to deal with the problem. His uncle, I mean.
Amelia Joane, it's our problem. And, I would remind you, our husbands' problem. And it's the charity's problem.
Joane (*sulking*) OK, forget it, if you don't want any help.
Amelia (*softer, relenting*) Darling, we can't let anyone else know about this—it's too dangerous. It's we who have to decide.

Rachel But what can we do?
Joane Not a lot, that I can see.
Amelia Well, there's one choice that's absolutely straightforward. Do we pay Wallis or not?
Joane We don't know how much she wants—except it's going to be a chunk!
Rachel Does it matter?
Amelia Rachel's right. I mean, it was never our money anyway. We could easily have lost ten million on a deal.
Joane We never lost.
Amelia We came close once or twice. When plans were changed, that we didn't know about.
Joane Yeh, but we were always in and out before it made any difference. So what are you saying, Amelia? We should pay that bush pig ten mil?
Rachel Why not, if that's the end of it?
Joane Because it won't be. Be real. With people like that, there's never an end.
Amelia I'm not so sure.
Joane What d'you mean?
Amelia That's not such a huge sum of money to you. You could spend it all shopping.
Joane I'd give it a go, darls. I've known Ken spend that much on some arty-farty picture that just hangs on the wall of a bank vault!
Amelia Yes, but this Wallis woman is no big spender. You could tell from the way she talked that she's always envied what she thinks is high society.
Joane So? She still wants her sling.

Rachel looks at her

Kickback.
Amelia So for someone of a modest background, what we're talking about is an enormous amount of money. They could live in comfort for the rest of their life.
Joane (*musing*) D'you know, I used to think like that once?
Rachel (*hopefully*) Maybe we could have some kind of contract?

Joane glares at this ridiculous suggestion, but Amelia considers the point

Amelia A contract would be meaningless on both sides. But remember, D L Wallis is a government officer in a position of trust—and corruption is a very serious matter…
Joane (*warming to the idea*) You mean some kind of once-and-for-all payment?
Amelia Exactly. Fully documented. So that thereafter she could choose a life of luxury…

Act II, Scene 2

Joane Or a life sentence in jail.
Amelia If she were exposed, precisely.
Joane I like it. We'd be exposed too but it'd be almost worth it.
Rachel (*pained*) Don't say things like that, Joane.
Joane (*ignoring her*) But where do we get the wonga?
Rachel I wish you wouldn't keep using those Australian expressions.
Joane (*hurt*) It's not Oz, it's Pom. Wonga, cash, the hard stuff. Anyway, what I'm saying is, it still means raiding the charity.
Amelia Well, yes and no.
Rachel What does that mean?
Amelia Last night, by sheer chance, I heard about a massive takeover bid being prepared by one of my husband's companies. If we bought options now, we could probably earn enough to make that one-off payment to Wallis and still reach our original target. And then we're out, completely. What d'you say?
Joane Great idea. Call Salzburg.
Amelia Rachel?
Rachel (*in a brave but quivering voice*) Go for it.
Amelia All right. But before I do that, I've got to get hold of Wallis——
Joane (*interjecting*) Rather you than me.
Amelia —and make a meeting for tomorrow—and hope we've judged this right.
Rachel This will be the last time, won't it?
Amelia I told you. Joane, you've got to call Carlo, stop his uncle from sticking his oar in. This is something we've got to clear up ourselves.
Joane Yeh, OK. I'm seeing him later.

Rachel gives her a reproving look. Joane just glares back

Amelia (*with a deep breath*) Right. Here we go then. (*She moves to the phone*) May I?
Rachel You're welcome.

Amelia checks the number on the card and punches it in. Rachel and Joane watch her expectantly

Amelia (*in her most regal manner*) Hallo? Securities and Exchange Commission?

Black-out

Scene 3

Next day, midday

Lighting indicates the different time of day, as does a change of scarf, belt or hat where appropriate, to suggest another costume

Amelia paces the room angrily, watched by Rachel

Amelia Bloody woman. She was supposed to be here at twelve o'clock. What does she think she's playing at? And where the hell's Joane?
Rachel (*tentatively*) I guess with, you know...
Amelia You mean Carlo—who else? (*She moves to the phone*) I'm going to ring and find out what's delaying Wallis.
Rachel OK.

Amelia checks the card, keys the number

Amelia D L Wallis please. ... (*with some irritation as if the receptionist is not hearing her properly*) D L Wallis! (*She cups the phone. To Rachel*) I didn't have this problem getting through yesterday.... Yes, hallo? ... (*She frowns*) I'm just a friend. Who are you? (*She listens, grows uncomfortable*) We were going to have lunch today, that's all. I met her when she was in London last week. Look, d'you mind telling me what this is all about? ... She what? ... When? ... Oh, my God. ... No, no, it was just social ... we only met recently ... thank you. (*She looks quite pale as she puts down the receiver*)
Rachel Amelia! What's happened?
Amelia D L Wallis didn't come into the office this morning.
Rachel Well, that doesn't mean anything.
Amelia (*slumping into a chair*) Her car was fished out of the Hudson River at eleven a.m.

The intercom rings. Rachel moves to answer it

Rachel Hallo? ... Yes. (*She replaces the receiver*) It's Joane. (*She returns to their conversation*) Was she hurt bad?
Amelia That's the weird thing. She wasn't in the car.
Rachel (*uncertainly*) Well, it was an accident. Maybe she managed to get out. She might have been a strong swimmer...
Amelia Rachel, even I know you don't go swimming in the Hudson River, not in December. And if she did manage to get out, someone would have known by now.

Act II, Scene 3   43

The sound of a ping from the elevator in the hall

Rachel (*moving to the exit*) This is terrible.

Rachel exits to the hall

Amelia (*to herself, thoughtfully*) That's one way of looking at it.

Rachel enters, followed by Joane, who does not apologize, just looks at them both

They look back. Rachel looks to Amelia, waiting for her to explain to Joane, but Joane speaks first

Joane You know?
Amelia (*after a pause*) What d'you mean, do we know?
Joane (*guiltily*) Oh...
Rachel (*genuinely bewildered*) How could you know...?
Amelia This wouldn't have anything to do with Carlo, would it? Or his uncle?
Joane I tried to stop him.
Rachel Doing what?
Joane But I was too late.

They both look at her

　　　He said he'd taken care of it. Uncle Mario.
Amelia Oh, marvellous. As if long sentences for fraud weren't enough, we're now accomplices to murder!
Rachel What're you saying, Amelia? I couldn't go to prison. I've got Benjie——
Joane (*interrupting*) What d'you mean, murder?
Amelia I mean D L Wallis's car was dragged from the river this morning. Admittedly, there was no D L Wallis in it...

Joane collapses into a chair with a sigh

Joane That's all right, then ... they can't prove murder.
Amelia What's that got to do with it? The body can still be found, you know. This is your responsibility, Joane.
Joane (*aggressively*) Listen, you don't know half about that Wallis woman. She's been blackmailing a lot of guys. And left a couple of suicides in her wake...

Rachel (*faintly*) Oh my... I cannot believe this!
Amelia (*holding her head in her hands*) All right! It's over now! (*She drops her hands*) It is over?
Rachel (*firmly, for once*) Oh, yes!
Joane Er—not quite.
Rachel No...?
Amelia Tell me.
Joane Er... well, Uncle Mario——
Amelia (*scathing*) Dear Uncle Mario.
Joane —wondered if we could do him a small favour in return.
Amelia He wants us to kill someone?
Joane (*laughing*) No, no... (*Her laughter rings hollowly*)

The others are stony-faced

Amelia What?
Joane He wants nothing from us—really. In fact, he wants to give us something.
Amelia No, thanks.
Joane A loan.
Amelia We don't need a loan.
Joane To the charity.
Amelia What for?
Joane I dunno. He just wants to make us a loan of ten million dollars.

They both look at her

   That's all.
Amelia At a premium?
Joane No interest.
Amelia He wants nothing back at all?
Joane Absolutely nothing. Just the money, of course. In non-dollar hard currencies.

Amelia covers her face with her hands

Amelia Oh, no...
Joane (*defensively*) What's so wrong with that?
Rachel (*perplexed*) No-one wants to trade dollars.

Amelia drags her hands down from her face

Amelia I'm afraid some people do, my dear. Do forgive me but when I

Act II, Scene 4

mentioned our conspiracy in fraud and suspected murder, I forgot to mention laundering money for the Mafia.

Joane starts to answer, thinks the better of it

Rachel You mean, like *The Godfather*?
Amelia Probably worse.
Joane (*angrily*) Listen, they're nice people...
Rachel (*fairly*) They do have family values.
Amelia I just hope our husbands do too. Or you can add the divorce courts—and that's when we come out of prison. If they wait.
Joane Uncle Mario says it'll all be covered up. When the SEC find out about Wallis, it'll just be an embarrassment for them.
Amelia Have you thought they may find out about us?
Rachel Oh, I hope Harry never knows about this. He gets so stressed, you know. It would almost kill him.
Joane I hope Ken never does. He'd almost kill me.

They all stand staring at each other dismally as the Lights fade to Black-out

Scene 4

The apartment in Sydney. Morning the next day

Ken is handing out drinks to Harry and Sir John. In Australia, at this time of the year, it is warm and the men are in shirtsleeves. Ken has a certain kind of veneer when it comes to dealing with respectable business colleagues

Ken Gentlemen, thank you for coming. It's a long way, I know, but security-wise, it's the safest place.
Harry Where's safe anymore? You've been hit as badly as we have.
Ken That's right and I know we've all been making our own enquiries... that's what we're here for, to compare notes, to try and solve this thing.
John (*somewhat suspiciously*) All right—what've you found out?
Ken (*shrugging*) The same as you, I guess. My corporate activities have been under close scrutiny, as have yours. (*To Harry*) And yours. But—and this is a big but—apparently no-one else's.
John It's infuriating. There must have been hundreds of companies involved, thousands of transactions...
Ken But only one common element. Everything, in the end, comes back to me, or you. (*To Harry*) Or you.
Harry You don't know what troubles I've had with the SEC...

John It's not just the SEC—there have been various investigating agencies, apparently all coming to the same conclusion...
Ken That we're in cahoots.
Harry I had this terrible woman always sniffing around...
Ken Who just had a nasty accident...
John This D L Wallis, you mean? They're treating that incident with suspicion too.
Harry Which means they think we're responsible!
John Preposterous! As if I'd be involved in anything like that!
Harry Or me.
Ken (*after a pause*) Yeh, well ... what we cannot get away from, gentlemen, is the fact we've been bracketed together in this.
John But why? (*To Ken, unable to conceal his dislike*) I mean, why should we be suspected of doing business together?
Harry Yeh, that's the question.
Ken And that's why we haven't been able to find the answer. Because that was the wrong question to ask. But there is a common link we share.
Harry We do?
John You mean our wives? That charity thing?
Harry Oh, yeh...
Ken And, so far as I know, that's the only thing. (*He moves to the window, to look out*) Now ain't that a coincidence?
John Well, yes, but that's all it is. You're surely not suggesting...?
Harry (*genuinely amused*) My Rachel? You got to be kidding.
John Even if they would do such a thing— (*he chuckles at the thought*) and Amelia probably would ... they couldn't!

Ken turns to face them both

Ken Not on their own. But a number of different small companies—all trading out of Salzburg—have made killings on our operations.
John Well, we know that.
Ken Let me ask you a question, Sir John. Have you been tapped by your wife recently?
John If you mean have I been asked for donations to charity... (*He thinks*) As a matter of fact, no.
Ken And is that unusual?
John Well ... yes...
Ken Harry?
Harry The answers are no and yes, like Sir John. But what does that prove?
Ken All right, let me tell you something else. The Save Our Starving Campaign, which pretty well lives from hand-to-mouth—or did—has a *very* substantial bank balance at the moment...

Act II, Scene 4

John (*mystified as to where all this is going*) Well, that would explain why we haven't been asked for money.
Ken It explains more than that. The campaign's received some big donations from certain companies——
Harry Rachel's a good fund-raiser.
Ken You didn't let me finish. From certain companies market-trading out of Salzburg?
John (*after a pause*) Oh my God... But they couldn't... How could they?
Harry Oh, come on, this has been some really smart guy, who knows how to operate...
Ken Fairly smart, yeh. But what he really needs to know is where to get information. He may even be just a front, doing what he's told. They're not playing the markets themselves.
John Then what are they doing?
Ken Providing that information?

Sir John throws his arms in the air at this absurd idea

John Oh...!
Harry Don't tell me this. Please.
John Insider trading?
Ken That's my guess.
Harry Please. Do not use those words. (*He rubs the pit of his stomach. He is in pain*)
John But how?
Ken Well... I had to rack my brains about that, I must admit...
John And?
Ken Have either of you noticed your wives taking maybe just a little more interest in your work, as of late?
John (*as the thought strikes him*) Oh, my...
Harry You know, it's funny you should say that...
Ken Well, I have. And since normally, Joane doesn't give a sh—a fig—about what I'm doing, not work-wise anyways, when she did, I noticed.
John Have you spoken to her?
Ken Not yet.
John Are you going to? And would she admit it?
Ken (*after a pause*) I'll persuade her.
Harry Look, this is crazy. OK, Rachel's been asking a few questions lately, but only because she's teaching Benjie what Daddy does at work... (*He tries to laugh it off*) You guys don't know Rachel...
John (*thoughtfully*) I'm beginning to wonder just how well any of us know our wives.
Ken It's not a case to take to court, but we're not going to do that anyway, so let's take a gander at the evidence ourselves. They're all involved in this

charity. They're passionate about raising money for it. Then someone comes up with an idea...
Harry Yeh, but who? (*Always self-centred*) Who would do this to me?

They both look at him

Or to you...?
Ken (*growling*) Well, obviously I don't know who, it might be the bloody Bishop of Walworth, or whatever they call him. But someone did. (*He spells out his case convincingly*) All they have to do is keep their eyes and ears open, pick up any odd bits of information that come their way.
Harry No, no, no. My Rachel couldn't have any part in this. She doesn't even like me talking business at home, she's told me a hundred times.
Ken Do you keep a personal computer there? I mean something that's really personal?
Harry Sure I do. Where d'you think I've been trying to hide this last three months? I wouldn't trust anyone else but me.
Ken And did your wife major in computer studies? At Columbia?
Harry (*angrily*) How d'you know this?
Ken Because I checked on you. Everything about you.
Harry Me? You think I'm a crook?
Ken Sure.
Harry Well, it takes one to know one.
John Gentlemen, please.
Ken Anyway, you were the first person I suspected. Until I saw you were in deep yourself. Sir John? What about you.
John (*after a pause*) My wife has always given me the impression that she never listens to a word I say.
Ken Exactly. We've all been suckered into this. And now we've got to get out of it.
John We've still got to challenge them.
Ken Right, and I suggest we all do it at roughly the same time—morning here, afternoon in New York, evening in the UK.
John So there's no conferring?

Ken nods

Right, synchronize watches...

John and Ken both check their watches. Harry's mind is elsewhere

Harry Yeh, but then what?

They both look at him

Act II, Scene 5   49

I mean, if you're right about this ... what do we do then? (*He is appalled*)

Ken looks brutal. Sir John's face gives nothing away

A pause

John What indeed?

Black-out

SCENE 5

The New York apartment. Afternoon the same day

Joane rises, to end the conversation, as do Amelia and Rachel

Joane I have to go. Ken wants me in Sydney, I don't know why—some society bash, I s'pose. Tough titty. I won't be staying.
Rachel Will you be coming back to New York?
Joane Oh yeh, you bet... Carlo and I are going to live here...
Amelia You're leaving Ken?

Joane nods

Rachel (*uncertainly*) Oh dear...
Amelia Then why are you going back?
Joane Tie up loose ends. Get a divorce...
Rachel I think that's a real pity...
Amelia It's a final step.
Joane It's one I've got to take—if I'm gonna marry Carlo...
Rachel (*in a different tone*) You're getting married?
Joane Yeh ... he insisted... I told him he was crazy ... but in the end I gave in.
Amelia Darling...

Amelia embraces her and so does Rachel. Although Joane tries to make light of it, she is obviously very happy

Rachel You see... I told you...
Amelia What did you tell us?
Rachel Italians believe in the family...
Joane (*reflectively*) Yeh, they do that all right. And by the way, I've already

had my wedding present from Uncle Mario—exactly what I asked for. You can forget about the money laundering...
Amelia Phew! That's a relief.

Joane prepares to go

Let us know how you get on, won't you?
Joane Sure. I'll get back real late tonight but I've already told Ken, I want to see him tomorrow—and before he buggers off to work.
Rachel Harry's coming back in the morning. He's been in New Zealand, I think he said. He's going straight to the office but he'll be back early, some time in the afternoon.
Amelia Well, that's comforting for you, isn't it? I never know where my husband is—I see him when I see him. (*To Joane*) Hang on, I might as well come with you. I'm going back tonight, via Paris.
Rachel No direct flights?
Amelia Oh, yes—I just want to visit my hairdresser.
Joane Nice one.
Amelia I'll be home tomorow evening. (*She moves to kiss Rachel*) Darling ... goodbye...
Rachel Wow! I'll miss you, Amelia...

Joane kisses Rachel

Amelia (*smiling*) Never mind, you've always got Benjie...
Joane (*to Rachel*) See you, darls.
Rachel You take care now, both of you.

Amelia and Joane move towards the door, then pause

Amelia (*slipping her gloves on*) Well ... fingers crossed... (*She beams*) I think we may have got away with it.

Black-out

Scene 6

The apartment in Sydney. Next day, morning

There is a dangerous tension about Ken as he prowls around the apartment

Joane is wearing a robe. She is nervous but resolute

Act II, Scene 6   51

Ken I ought to kick your ass right out of here.
Joane Fine.
Ken Oh, no—you're not going to get away that easy. You nearly ruined me.
Joane Oh, bull dust. You know, you're a real old drama queen, Stocksie. You must have got it from that actress you were shacking up with. I didn't ruin you. I didn't do anything to you. I may have stopped you and that bunch of rat-bags and bludgers you call your business associates from robbing some widows and orphans, but that's all.
Ken (*angrily*) You did all right out of it.
Joane Me? No. Come off it, sport. Every penny we made has gone, or will go, to the charity.
Ken (*greedily*) You mean you've still got money left?
Joane If we have, or we haven't, you're not having it.
Ken We'll see about that. (*He glowers at her*) You know, you want a bloody good hiding.
Joane No, I don't. And I never did. It just gave you some kind of perverse pleasure to give me one. But not any more, Ken, that's over.
Ken Don't bet on it. If I treated you so bad, why didn't you leave?
Joane Do you think I didn't try? I've walked out of this door, or that door, wherever we were living, a hundred times. And I've always come back.
Ken (*sneering*) You haven't got the bottle.
Joane Oh, yes, I have. You'll see I have. You just don't get it, do you, you thick-headed bull? The only reason I came back was because I loved you. The only reason I put up with all your dirty shenanigans was because I loved you. But that's finished now.
Ken You tried to make a fool out of me.
Joane I didn't have to do that, you made a fool of yourself. Oh, you're clever all right, in your own way, too clever for your own good sometimes. What was it they used to call you one time, the Melbourne Midas? Sure, everything you touched turned to gold—and then you turned it into dross. I've had enough, Ken. I'm leaving.
Ken You're not going anywhere unless I tell you to go. (*He threateningly slips off his belt and wraps it round his fist*)

Joane does not flinch

Joane (*quietly*) I want a divorce.
Ken I've told you before——
Joane Yes, I know. It'd be cheaper for you to have me knocked off. Well, it won't cost you anything. I'm just taking a few personal possessions, and that's it.

Ken is uneasy: he is beginning to believe she means what she is saying.

Previous rows have just been passionate brawls, mud-slinging matches. Ken is unused to a calm and determined Joane and does not know how to react. So he blusters, as he always does

Ken What d'you mean, you want a divorce? You don't get a divorce unless I say so.
Joane Yes, I do. I've got tons of evidence, mate. You want to wash your dirty linen in public? The newspapers would love it—and you don't own them all… Come to think of it, it would give your rivals a chance to get back at you.
Ken Oh yeh? Dog doesn't eat dog.
Joane I think you'll find they do, if they're dingos. But let's do each other a favour, eh? We'll just let this go through nice and quiet—no faults claimed on either side, no statements to the press, just an amicable parting. What d'you say?
Ken I say, screw you.
Joane Very eloquent. Is that yes, or no?

Ken is completely thrown by this conversation. He is raging about the room now like an angry and frustrated animal

Ken What do I care? Listen, if you've got some bloody toyboy in tow, then keep him—but keep him out of sight. I don't want to know about.
Joane It's not like that, Ken. I love him.

The simple conviction of her words brings him to a halt

Ken You said you love me!
Joane I said I loved you.

Ken is again like an entrapped animal that doesn't know where to move

Ken Well, all right, I know I've been a bit of a roustabout lately…
Joane (*correcting him*) A nong.
Ken Yeh…
Joane A dill.
Ken Yeh, OK…
Joane A galah.
Ken I told you before, I just get lonely sometimes…
Joane No, you don't.
Ken Well, cripes, I'm just a man—some of these judies throw themselves at you!
Joane Ken—it doesn't matter any more.

Act II, Scene 6 53

Ken (*almost desperately*) I can change.
Joane No. You can't change anything. But I can. And that's why I'm going.
Ken (*getting angry again*) You're bloody not... (*He advances towards her, threatening*)
Joane Don't even try it, Ken.
Ken You want to walk out on me? I'll give you something to bloody remember me by.

Joane dodges behind furniture as he circles the room after her

Joane Carlo won't like it...
Ken Carlo's not going to get it. Not yet, anyway. What is he, an effing eyetie?

Joane makes a last desperate throw of the dice as Ken pursues her

Joane His name's Carlo Galenti, Ken. His uncle's Mario Galenti. The family owns casinos in Las Vegas.

Ken comes to a halt, reason struggling with emotion

> You know the name, don't you? Ken, do yourself a favour. Don't mess with the Galenti family. They're in a different league.

Ken makes a last show of bravado

Ken You think I'm scared of that lot?
Joane If you're not, you ought to be. You know they're here, don't you? In this city? That's how I came to meet Carlo.

Ken knows full well that what she is saying makes sense. He is part of the criminal fraternity himself, posing behind legitimate enterprises, and these people are arch rivals. The bluster deflates

Ken It's not true, Jo. I've always loved you. I know I've been a bit rough sometimes...
Joane More than a bit.
Ken And I've done some bad things...
Joane A lot of bad things.
Ken But we've been together a long time now...
Joane Maybe too long...
Ken And we've had some good times—haven't we?
Joane (*after a pause*) It's hard to remember.
Ken (*with great difficulty*) I can't live without you, Jo...

Joane (*looking at him*) You should have thought of that before.
Ken (*getting angry again*) I mean it... (*He makes a threatening step towards her*) And I'm not going to let anyone else——

Ken's tirade is cut off by the sound of the phone ringing, as Joane retreats anxiously before him. Ken blinks, as though awakened from a dream. The phone is within Joane's reach. She picks it up

Joane (*into the phone*) Hallo? Oh, Carlo, hi...

Ken stands glaring at her, his emotions in turmoil again

>No, everything's fine. ... No, I'm sure Ken's going to be reasonable about this...

She looks directly at Ken

>That's right, it's an offer he can't refuse. OK, you'll meet me at the airport like we planned. ... No, I won't be late. I'm leaving right away. ... Yeh, promise. OK, bye... (*She puts the phone down*) That was just for insurance purposes, Ken. You know what I mean? So you better make sure I don't turn up crook—he wouldn't like that. Nor would Uncle Mario. (*She moves towards the door*)

Ken stays in the same spot, swivelling to watch her. He holds out his hand, unaware that he still carries his belt. There is no threat in the gesture at all. It is a plea for help

Ken (*hoarsely*) Jo...

Joane shakes her head

Joane It's over, Ken. You're history, mate, history.

>*Joane goes out, leaving Ken stunned*

Black-out

Scene 7

The Milchans' apartment in New York. A grey afternoon the same day

Rachel is just emerging from the door that leads to Benjie's room. She calls out behind her

Rachel Poppa will be right with you, Benjie. But he's tired, it's been a long flight.

We hear the sound of the elevator's distinctive ping

Rachel checks her hair in the mirror and turns to greet a dismal Harry as he enters

She helps him off with his scarf and greatcoat

Harry (*shuddering*) Is this winter never going to end?
Rachel If you're cold, I'll get the heating turned up.
Harry No, no, I'll be all right now. (*Tragically*) It's the cold inside, Rachel.
Rachel Is it the flu? Should I call Doctor Weitzmann?
Harry No. (*He starts to pace about the room*) It's nothing physical.
Rachel You're sure?
Harry I'm certain.
Rachel Oh, good. Then why don't you go and see Benjie, so he stops fretting, and then we can relax and you can tell me about your trip.
Harry I don't want to see Benjie!
Rachel Oh! OK. I told him you'd be tired. Maybe you can read him a bedtime story later. Would you like a drink, honey?
Harry Yes, I would. I would very much like a drink.
Rachel Is there something wrong, dear?
Harry There is something that is—cataclysmically awfully—wrong!

Rachel begins to get his drift. She moves to get the drink

Rachel Oh, wow!
Harry (*bitterly*) Yes, God help us all, wow! (*He sinks into a chair*) Am I mistaken, Rachel, did you once make a vow to love and honour me always?
Rachel (*bringing him his drink*) I do love you, sweety-pie, you know that.
Harry It is the honour section of the contract that bothers me, sweetheart. Have you brought dishonour on me and my business associates, that is what I need to know. Have you lost me points on my credit rating in Wall Street? In a single word—have you betrayed me?

This last speech has hardened Rachel's attitude. She is prepared to argue now

Rachel You mean, with a man?
Harry No, I do not mean with a man.
Rachel You'd prefer that, wouldn't you?

Harry almost falls into the trap

Harry Ye— (*He just pulls himself up in time*) Do not try and turn this round, Rachel. You know what I am talking about.
Rachel (*quite tough*) Sure. You're talking about a lurk, as Joane would call it, a scheme we thought up to make a little wonga.
Harry A what!?
Rachel A little money.
Harry A little money!
Rachel Don't lose your hair about it—it's peanuts to you.
Harry (*apoplectically*) I can't afford to lose——
Rachel (*interrupting*) You lost nothing. You just didn't make, that's all. And don't tell me you can't afford it. You've got zillions!
Harry (*indignantly*) Hey, it's not just my money, you know. It's yours. It's Benjie's!
Rachel I don't want it. And I don't want Benjie to have it.
Harry (*shaken to the core*) You can't mean that!
Rachel I can. I do. Can't you see, Harry? Benjie doesn't need your money, he needs you.
Harry (*protesting*) I'm going to read him a bedtime story, I said I would.
Rachel Oh sure. You know what happens—it's always the same. By the time you arrive, he's fast asleep.
Harry You want me to wake him up?
Rachel (*with passion*) I want you to see him in the morning—not go off to work before he opens his eyes. I want you to see him in the evening, and not late at night when he's tired. And I want you to see him during the day sometimes, and at weekends. I want you to take him to ball-games, buy him popcorn, go to the movies with him, do all the things regular poppas do.
Harry (*genuinely upset*) How can you say these things to me, Rachel? Don't you think I love you and Benjie, more than my life?
Rachel No, Harry. You love your life more than us. I don't doubt you wouldn't die for us. But you wouldn't pass up on a good deal.

Harry passes a hand across his brow

Harry I don't understand. Am I crazy? Who was the victim here?

Act II, Scene 8   57

Rachel Maybe we're all victims. I know I did wrong in the eyes of the law. If I have to be punished for it, that's OK. But at least it was an experience that taught me something, Harry. I found out a lot about your world. And I also found out that you know nothing, and care nothing, about my life.

Harry, broken now, stands up. He has tears in his eyes

Harry How can you say that to me, Rachel? That I don't care?

We hear the sound of Benjie's voice calling out, muffled

Benjie's Voice Pop-pa... Pop-pa...
Rachel (*quite hard now*) Are you going in to see your son, Harry?
Harry (*choking back his tears*) I'm going. (*He calls out*) Coming, Benj. Coming...

But first he throws himself in Rachel's arms, weeping. Melting immediately, she weeps too, but with joy, caressing him

The Lights fade to Black-out

SCENE 8

The Belgravia mansion in London. Evening the same day

Amelia stands C in contemplation

Sir John watches her from across the room

Amelia You wouldn't really report me to the Stock Exchange?
John I'd have to take advice on that. Perhaps the Crown Prosecution Service.
Amelia (*incredulously*) Me? Your wife?
John Would you have been so self-righteously indignant if you had committed murder? Or robbery? Which indeed you have.
Amelia Oh, rubbish. All we've done is take a few quid from the rich to give to the poor, which Robin Hood used to do all the time.
John It was rather more than a few quid and you are not Robin Hood. He was never entitled to redistribute wealth anyway, and he certainly wouldn't be under this government.
Amelia (*impatiently*) What you lost was nothing to you.
John That is not the point, Amelia. I am not talking about money...
Amelia Oh, good.

John I am talking about principles.
Amelia Oh, God.
John You seem to forget my position.
Amelia Well, you seem to forget mine. I bet Harry Milchan's not threatening to shop his wife.
John That is entirely up to him.
Amelia I bet even Ken Stocks won't. Mind you, she knows too much about his past.
John Again, that is up to them. Though I must tell you, if your presumptions are correct, that present secrecy will not render them immune from future prosecution.
Amelia Oh, you can be so stuffy sometimes, John.
John I have a position to uphold. It is essential that the integrity of that position is protected. The City exists on its reputation for honourable trading...
Amelia You're more than stuffy, you're insufferable. At times like this, John, let me tell you, I find you a prig, a bore and a hypocrite. In fact, what Joane would call a drongo!
John You can be as vituperative as you like...
Amelia (*scathingly*) The City! It's a greedy little boys' club. All out to make as much as they can get and if someone else wants a bit of it—even for a worthy cause—they all scream foul play.

This is not going the way Sir John had hoped. Even so, he preserves his strict demeanour

John (*loftily*) Nevertheless...
Amelia (*interrupting*) All right then, do it. Report me!
John You just don't see, do you? I have no choice.
Amelia It won't get you off the hook, you know. They're bound to think you were involved.
John That is nonsense. I am on record as expressing my abhorrence at this rogue trading. The City, at my personal instigation, has launched a rigorous investigation...
Amelia Well, it didn't get far, did it? The SEC were well ahead of your lot.
John (*concerned*) What do you know about the SEC's involvement?
Amelia All you need to know is they're not taking any action—one of their own agents was on the take.
John (*aghast*) You bribed somebody?
Amelia We bribed no-one. But I have it on good authority that the SEC's embarrassed and they're prepared to let the matter drop—so why can't you?
John Because we are not compromised. The City authorities have no reason for embarrassment.

Act II, Scene 8   59

Amelia (*appealing to his good sense*) John, it's over now. We have closed the offices in Salzburg...
John I have questions about Salzburg too.
Amelia We've stopped trading. All the money has been transferred to the charity...
John That does not close the matter.

Amelia is getting really fed up now

Amelia I see—so you're above it all, are you?
John I certainly wasn't involved in any way...
Amelia And no mud will stick?
John Why should it?
Amelia And you'll send me to prison?
John That is a matter for the law. But, as you've made no personal gain, and if restitution is made, a judge might take a lenient view. Of course, as for your fellow conspirators...
Amelia You mean Rachel and Joane?
John They come under their own jurisdictions. I was referring to whoever physically did this trading on your behalf...
Amelia Ah! That's what you're after, is it? A convenient scapegoat?
John Leave it to the lawyers, Amelia. They will know the best thing to do. (*He reaches out a hand awkwardly*) And I'll stand by you.

But Amelia is having none of it. She refuses to let him touch her

Amelia Right. So you come out of this smelling of roses, for reporting me?
John I wouldn't put it like that.
Amelia It's all down to me, and Rachel and Joane? We were acting entirely independently?
John You were.
Amelia So you couldn't possibly be involved?
John Not directly. How could I be?
Amelia And so the poor trader we employed has to take all the blame?
John That's the best way out of this mess, Amelia, believe me. Who is he, by the way?
Amelia What makes you think it's a he?
John (*taken aback*) Well, who?
Amelia Gerry. Your daughter.

Long pause

John What? (*He does not really believe this*)

Amelia Why are you so surprised?
John Geraldine!
Amelia She likes to be called Gerry. You always said she was a clever girl.
John I don't believe it.

Amelia goes towards one of the doors and calls out

Amelia Gerry, you can come in now... (*To John*) Sorry, Geraldine.

Gerry enters. She looks quite different now. Demurely dressed and with a neat hair style, she could be any bright young City girl

John collapses in a chair, gazing at her open-mouthed

Gerry Hallo, Dad...
Amelia He'll say hallo in a moment, darling, when he's stopped gasping for air. (*To John*) So you see, my love, it all looks a bit different now, doesn't it? With me as the prime mover of this wicked scheme and your daughter as Chief Executive, I'd say some mud would stick—wouldn't you?

Sir John is still having trouble with his breathing

John I—don't—understand...
Amelia It's quite simple. Gerry wanted to go off with her young man and you wouldn't let her. And you took all her money away so they were penniless, which meant she had to get a job. And it so happened I had a job going—in Salzburg. Killed two birds with one stone, really. (*To Gerry*) How is Paul, darling?

Sir John watches the following exchange as though he were at a tennis match

Gerry He dumped me. For some Austrian girl. But I'm in love with Jean-Paul now and we want to get married. You'll love him.
Amelia Another artist?
Gerry (*wrinkling her nose*) A merchant banker, I'm afraid. But he's cool. We're both into ecology.
John (*in a strangled voice; to Gerry*) A merchant banker?
Amelia Yes, dear, but I think she ought to put off the marriage till she comes out of prison.

Sir John rises, stands swaying tragically

John How can I send my only daughter to prison?

Act II, Scene 8

Amelia The same way you were going to send your only wife, dear.
John (*turning fiercely on her*) Amelia, you always do this to me! You always make me seem in the wrong, somehow!
Amelia (*innocently*) Do I? Well, let's talk about it at dinner. I'll see what Mrs Jenkins has rustled up for us. But you should take a little rest first ... perhaps a little Valium, too. (*She takes John's arm and starts to guide him off*) Excuse your father, darling, he's had a hard day...

Amelia and John exit

Gerry moves c and breathes a giant sigh of relief just as Amelia returns

Gerry Phew!!
Amelia Are you all right, dear?
Gerry (*grinning*) I'll be glad to get rid of these silly clothes. What are you up to today?
Amelia I have a luncheon.
Gerry Still saving the starving?

Sir John comes wandering back as she answers, just in time to catch the tail end of their conversation

Amelia (*with enthusiasm*) Of course. And I have another wonderful idea!

In a brief moment of unity, father and daughter both wince as——

—*the* CURTAIN *falls*

FURNITURE AND PROPERTY LIST

Further dressing may be added at the director's discretion. See also Production Note on p. xi and Author's Note (p. vii)

ACT I

Prologue

On stage: Screen or monitor (where applicable)

Scene 1

Set: Armchair
Phone

Strike: Screen or monitor

Off stage: **John**'s covert coat and bowler (**Mary**)

Personal: **John:** glasses, wallet, watch (worn throughout)

Scene 2

Set: *Financial Times* newspaper

Scene 3

Re-set: Phone

Set: Various items of furniture

Strike: Armchair
Financial Times newspaper

Off stage: Boxes from expensive London shops, containing clothes (**Joane**)

Furniture and Property List

Scene 4

Re-set:	Phone
Set:	Intercom Chair Notes
Strike:	Various items of furniture Boxes from expensive London shops
Personal:	**Joane:** watch (worn throughout)

Scene 5

Re-set:	Phone
Set:	Armchair
Strike:	Intercom Chair Notes
Off stage:	Visiting card (**Mary**)

ACT II

Scene 1

On stage:	Armchair Phone Visiting card
Personal:	**Wallis:** notebook **Amelia:** visiting card

Scene 2

Re-set:	Phone
Set:	Intercom Chair

Strike: Armchair

Personal: **Amelia:** visiting card

Scene 3

On stage: As before

Personal: **Amelia:** visiting card

Scene 4

Re-set: Phone

Set: Various items of furniture
            Glasses with drinks

Strike: Intercom
            Chair

Personal: **Ken:** watch

Scene 5

Re-set: Phone

Set: Intercom
            Chair

Strike: Various items of furniture
            Glasses with drinks

Scene 6

Re-set: Phone

Set: Various items of furniture

Strike: Intercom
            Chair

Personal: **Ken:** belt

Furniture and Property List 65

SCENE 7

Re-set: Phone

Set: Intercom
Chair
Bottle containing drink
Glass

Strike: Various items of furniture

SCENE 8

Re-set: Phone

Set: Armchair

Strike: Intercom
Chair
Bottle containing drink
Glass

LIGHTING PLOT

Property fittings required: nil
1 interior. The same throughout

ACT I, PROLOGUE

To open: Overall general lighting

Cue 1   **Peter**: "…News at One."   (Page 2)
Black-out

ACT I, SCENE 1

To open: Late Autumn morning lighting

Cue 2   **Amelia** starts to leave the room   (Page 6)
Fade lights

ACT I, SCENE 2

To open: Brighter late Autumn morning lighting

Cue 3   **Amelia**: "My dear Bishop…"   (Page 15)
Black-out

ACT I, SCENE 3

To open: Early Summer evening lighting

Cue 4   **Joane**: "North Star… eh…?"   (Page 17)
Fade lights to Black-out

Lighting Plot

ACT I, SCENE 4

To open: Late Autumn evening lighting

Cue 5   **Rachel**: "Wow!"   (Page 28)
Black-out

ACT I, SCENE 5

To open: Late Autumn morning lighting

No cues

ACT II, SCENE 1

To open: Late Autumn morning lighting

Cue 6   **Wallis**: "That's all."   (Page 38)
Black-out

ACT II, SCENE 2

To open: Late Autumn morning lighting

Cue 7   **Amelia**: "Securities and Exchange Commission?"   (Page 41)
Black-out

ACT II, SCENE 3

To open: Late Autumn daylight

Cue 8   **Amelia, Joane**, and **Rachel** stare at each other   (Page 45)
Fade lights to Black-out

ACT II, SCENE 4

To open: Early Summer morning lighting

Cue 9   **John**: "What indeed?"   (Page 49)
Black-out

ACT II, SCENE 5

To open: Late Autumn afternoon lighting

Cue 10   **Amelia**: "I think we may have got away with it."   (Page 50)
            Black-out

ACT II, SCENE 6

To open: Early Summer morning lighting

Cue 11   **Joane** goes out, leaving **Ken** stunned   (Page 54)
            Black-out

ACT II, SCENE 7

To open: Early Winter grey afternoon lighting

Cue 12   **Harry** and **Rachel** weep   (Page 57)
            Fade lights to Black-out

ACT II, SCENE 8

To open: Early Winter evening lighting

No cues

EFFECTS PLOT

ACT I

Cue 1	To open Prologue *Display prologue action as script page 1*	(Page 1)
Cue 2	**Amelia**: "…in a million years. It's——" *Knock on the door*	(Page 14)
Cue 3	**Amelia**: "I can't wait to see that first plane loaded." *Sound of elevator's ping from hallway*	(Page 22)
Cue 4	**Joane**: "…together for a while and then——" *Knock on the door*	(Page 31)
Cue 5	**Amelia**: "Now!" *Phone rings, continuing*	(Page 32)
Cue 6	**Amelia** and **Joane** look at each other in horror *Knock on the door*	(Page 32)

ACT II

Cue 7	To open Scene 1 *Phone ringing*	(Page 33)
Cue 8	**Amelia**: "Just outlined the problem, she says." *Intercom rings*	(Page 38)
Cue 9	**Amelia**: "Nor do I." *Sound of elevator's ping from hallway*	(Page 39)
Cue 10	**Amelia**: "…out of the Hudson River at eleven a.m." *Intercom rings*	(Page 42)
Cue 11	**Amelia**: "…someone would have known by now." *Sound of elevator's ping from hall*	(Page 42)

Cue 12	**Ken**: "And I'm not going to let anyone else——" *Phone rings*	(Page 54)
Cue 13	**Rachel**: "But he's tired, it's been a long flight." *Sound of elevator's ping from hallway*	(Page 55)
Cue 14	**Harry**: "That I don't care?" **Benjie's Voice** *calling out, muffled, as script page 57*	(Page 57)